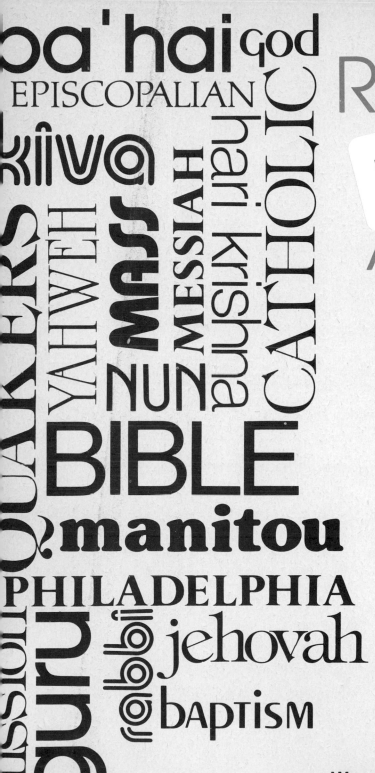

Religion in North America

Ronald J. Wilkins

wcb

Religious Education Division
Wm. C. Brown Company Publishers
Dubuque, Iowa

EDITORIAL CONSULTANTS

for *Sacred Scripture*—Very Rev. Brendan McGrath, Professor of Theology, Loyola University, Chicago, Illinois; Past President, the Catholic Biblical Association of America

for *Adolescent Religious Education*—Mrs. Ruth Cheney, Program Services Associate for the Youth Ministry of the Episcopal Church; former Chairman of the Screening Committee of the International Youth Exchange

for *Adolescent Psychology*—Dr. William D. Wilkins, Professor, School of Leadership and Human Behavior, United States International University, San Diego, California; Consultant for the Office of Economic Opportunity, Washington, D.C.

for *Social Sciences*—Dr. Raymond Polin, Professor of Political Science, Graduate School, St. John's University, Jamaica, L.I., New York

for *the Canadian Provinces*—Mr. John Quinn, Consultant for the Catholic Separate School Board, Diocese of Hamilton, Ontario, Canada

Fully aware of religious education as a key factor affecting human relations, the editors invited a Protestant and a Jewish scholar to review material presented in this book as it bears on their respective faith communities. These are Dr. Edward Zerin, Rabbi, and Dr. Martin E. Marty, Associate Editor, *Christian Century*. While their personal views and religious beliefs must obviously differ from some of the views presented, both feel that the content has been so handled as to increase intergroup understanding.

Scripture quotations in this publication are from the Today's English Version Bible—Old Testament: Copyright © American Bible Society 1976; New Testament: Copyright © American Bible Society 1966, 1971, 1976. Used by permission.

Excerpts from the Documents of Vatican II used by permission of the Publications Office of the United States Catholic Conference, Washington, D.C.

The author gratefully acknowledges the assistance of Ms. Marcy MacKinnon, Librarian, the Ecumenical Forum of Canada, Toronto, and Mrs. Ruth Tillman, Assistant Secretary, The Canadian Council of Churches, Toronto; Dolores Rogers and Dorothy Uttich, librarians, McHenry Public Library, McHenry, Illinois: Thomas and Catherine Crowley, Glenview, Illinois; Ms. Mary Lane, Skokie, Illinois, and Nancy Wilkins, McHenry, Illinois; Chris Kirsch, Paia, Maui, Hawaii; Fr. Dean Paleologus, Sts. Constantine and Helen Greek Orthodox Church, Palos Hills, Illinois; Bishop Willis Robinson, Ph.D., of Escondido, California; Rev. Roger W. Schneider, Shepherd of the Hills Lutheran Church, McHenry, Illinois; Rev. Ralph Smith, First United Methodist Church, McHenry, Illinois; Rev. Arthur McKay, St. Paul's Episcopal Church, McHenry, Illinois; and Rev. Michael Werry, First Baptist Church, McHenry, Illinois.

PHOTO-ILLUSTRATION CREDITS

Alaska Division of Tourism—27, 31, 165
Hal Bergsohn Associates—160
Grover Brinkman—117, 176, 178 (bottom), 179 (top center)
Craig M. Brown—cover, iv-1 (top)
Buechel Memorial Lakota Museum—40-1, 66, 68
David Burnett/CONTACT PRESS IMAGES—184 (bottom), 186-7
Camerique—6 (bottom), 82, 120-1
Ed Carlin—161
Church of Jesus Christ of Latter-day Saints—181, 184 (top)
Alan Cliburn—110-1
Colorado Division of Commerce and Development—iv (bottom left)
Bob Combs/FREEVISION—6, 18-9, 96-7, 100, 103, 134
Paul Conklin—13
Connecticut Department of Commerce—140
Culver Pictures—98 (bottom right)
Vivienne della Grotta—71
Bob Eckert/EKM—79
Elvehjem Art Center—166-7
Field Museum—38
Mimi Forsyth—72
David Frazier—54 (top), 141
David Hiebert—21
Dan Hubrich—8, 28, 95
Illinois Department of Conservation—179 (bottom)
Israel Ministry of Tourism—151
Jean-Claude LeJeune/STOCK MARKET—12
Library of Congress—178 (top), 179 (top), 182
Lick Observatory Photograph—22-3
Liedtkes of Dubuque—129, 133
Carolyn McKeone—4-5, 76, 85, 102, 107, 142-3, 145, 148, 157, 159, 189
Maine Department of Commerce and Industry—1 (bottom left)
Greg Mironchuk/MR ASSOCIATES—64, 70, 169
Museum of the American Indian—42
National Anthropological Archives, Smithsonian Institution—36
New York Convention and Visitor's Bureau—144
Richard Nowitz/NOVA—75, 172
Peabody Museum/M.W. Sexton—30, 32, 33
Philadelphia Convention and Visitor's Bureau—80, 126
Picture Archive—91, 92, 93, 138, 152
Religious News Service—1 (bottom right), 15 (top), 49, 51, 63, 69, 87, 88, 89, 90, 98-9, 109, 114, 115, 139, 158, 175, 180
Rhode Island Development Council—iv (bottom right), 81, 108, 154-5
San Diego Convention and Visitor's Bureau—46
Paul Schrock—14 (top), 30, 98 (top left), 101, 125
Florence Sharp—83
Springlife Studios—118, 128, 132, 137
L.S. Stepanowicz—14-5 (bottom), 47
Michael Sullivan—171
Swedish Information Service—122-3
Swiss National Tourist Office—52, 54 (bottom), 55 (top), 56-7, 59, 62, 73, 168
Paul Tick—16, 17, 190, 191
Jim Whitmer—119
Yugoslav Press and Cultural Center—55 (bottom), 67, 164
John Zielinski—11, 34, 94

CONTENTS

68629

An Introduction

Nothing is so universal in human experience as **religion.*** It cuts across the barriers of time, of race, of age, of civilizations, of economics, and of politics. It expresses a person's innermost feelings about himself and his perception of the world and goes to the very heart of his self-understanding.

It has shaped the personal and social lives of people ever since humanity emerged from its prehuman existence to its self-conscious awareness. It has helped forge the major civilizations and has influenced the economic, political,

---

*Words which appear in bold are defined in the glossary.

and cultural life of every society that has developed on earth. It has determined the course of history and of people's lives. Yet nothing, perhaps, is so misunderstood, neglected, and trivialized as the knowledge of what religion really is and what its role has been in developing the human condition. *Religion in North America* is written to help overcome this misunderstanding, neglect, and trivialization.

If religion is understood as a way of looking at reality and of relating to that reality, or as an attempt to relate to whatever God is for a person through signs, symbols, words, and acts, it can

Cliff Palace, Mesa Verde National Park, Cortez, Colorado

Touro Synagogue, Newport, Rhode Island

be seen that religion plays an important role in determining how people live out their lives and how society expresses its purpose. *Religion in North America* examines the signs, symbols, words, and acts of the religions that have shaped the lives and the history of the people of North America—in Canada, the United States, and Mexico. It is a source book for information on and discussions of the religious forces that have been and are a part of the North American scene.

It is impossible, of course, to detail each and every religion that has been or is now a part of the history of North America; therefore, *Religion in North America* will deal with the major religions and the major religious developments in North America. It will discuss the origin, principal beliefs, religious practices, and structures of each. It will focus its attention on what each religion discussed is and what it means for those who practice it.

It is hoped that through a study of religions in North America, the readers of *Religion in North America* will become more aware of the religious beliefs and practices of other Americans, will appreciate more their own religious roots, and will understand the heritage that makes the countries of North America unique in the family of nations.

Congregational Church, South Harpswell, Maine

Baha'i Temple, Wilmette, Illinois

1

ECSTASY
CULT
MORAL
MINISTERS ·LIFE
charism
death
RELIGION
atheist
·CATHOLIC CLERICAL CHRISTIANITY
MAGIC

The Present State of Religion in North America

North Americans are, by and large, a religious people. In the United States, for example, according to the *Gallup Opinion Index for 1977-78,* 94% of the people believe in God or a Universal Spirit, 68% describe themselves as members of some religious group, 60% say their religious beliefs are very important to them, and a majority believe that religion is having, and ought to have, a greater impact on both private and public affairs. According to the same poll, the figures for Canada are about the same as for the United States. In Mexico, well over 97% of the people are members of some religious group.

In the United States, 60% of the religious population is Protestant, 28% is Roman Catholic, 2% is Jewish, 4% belong to "other" religious groups, and 6% say they have no religious affiliation. Of the Protestant groups, 21% are Baptist, 11% are Methodist, 7% are Lutheran, 5% are Presbyterian, 3% are Episcopalian, and 13% are "other Protestant" such as the Congregationalists, the Disciples of Christ, and the Evangelical and Reformed Churches. In Canada, about

Estimated Membership in the Principal Religions in North America*

Roman Catholic	122,500,000	Mormon	3,500,000
Protestant	95,231,000	Oriental	310,000
Jewish	6,800,000	Moslem	250,000
Eastern Orthodox	4,500,000	New Religions	3,000,000

Total Population: 306,400,000

The Principal Religious Groups in North America
(Number of affiliated bodies in each group)

Adventist Churches (4)
Amana Church Society
Anglican Churches of Canada
Armenian Church of America
Assemblies of God
Baha'i
Baptist (27)
Berean Foundation
Bible Way Church of our Lord Jesus
   Christ Worldwide
Brethren (6)
Buddhist Churches of America
Christadelphians
Christian Missionary Alliance
Christian Church/Disciples of Christ
Christian Church of North America
Christian Nation Church, USA
Christian Union
Church of Christ (Holiness)
Church of Christ, Scientist
Church of God
Church of God in Christ
Church of the Nazarene
Churches of Christ
Churches of Christ in Christian Union
Churches of God (9)
Churches of the Living God (3)
Church of New Jerusalem
Congregational Christian Churches
Conservative Congregational
   Christian Churches
Eastern Orthodox Churches (25)
Evangelical Congregational Church
Evangelical Covenant Church
Evangelical Free Church
Evangelical Associations (4)
Free Christian Zion Church of Christ

Hindu
Independent Fundamentalist
   Churches of America
International Church of the
   Foursquare Gospel
Jehovah's Witnesses
Jewish Congregations (5)
Latter-day Saints (Mormon) (3)
Lutheran (11)
Mennonite (10)
Methodist (15)
Moravian (3)
Moslem
New Apostolic Church of North
   America
New Religion Cults (400)
Old Catholic Church (3)
Open Bible Standard Church
Pentecostal Assemblies (10)
Polish National Catholic Church
Presbyterian (10)
Protestant Episcopal
Quakers (Friends) (5)
Reformed Church (4)
Roman Catholic
Salvation Army
Shinto
Spiritualists (3)
Triumph the Church and Kingdom of
   God in Christ
Unitarian/Universalist
United Brethren (2)
United Church of Christ
Volunteers of America
Wesleyan Church
Worldwide Church of God

---

*No exact figure can be given because some Churches do not have current figures;
because other Churches variously list themselves as "Protestant" or "other"; and
because of the shifting population figures for various Oriental and Southeast Asian
peoples.

38% of the population is Protestant, 47% is Roman Catholic, 10% is "other," and 5% is "none." In Mexico, 93% of the population is Roman Catholic, 5% is "other," and 2% is "none."

Religion: Important to North Americans

The state of religion in North America is not measured by numbers alone. It is measured by its influence on people's lives, by its effect on society, and by its impact on cultural development. By these measurements, religion in North America is in a healthy state.

To some it may appear that religion does not seem to have as great an influence on North American life as it once had, but it does. There is a strong undercurrent of religious awareness and commitment in the peoples of North America, and the influence of religion is more pervasive than it was in the past. In earlier periods of North American history, religion had a marked institutional influence—often a particular denomination was the dominant force in establishing the religion, customs, mores, and political and social practices in a particular area. At the present time, however, especially in Canada and the United States, **religious pluralism** has tended to lessen the influence of one or another denomination, while at the same time it has increased the influence of religion in general. But although institutional religion may have

lost some of its power, the level of religious awareness is high and continues to influence North American culture. Therefore, while the nature of religious influence on North American society has changed, the influence itself remains vigorous because most people in North America are religiously aware to a greater or lesser degree.

At the present time, more and more people in North America are turning to spiritual values to give meaning to their lives. They are rejecting the unfulfilled and unrealistic promises ascribed to science, that science alone could not bring to pass. They are finding that exclusively **materialistic** goals are not

People are turning more and more toward the spirit—toward personal prayer, a deeper relationship to whatever God is for them, and to a religion that satisfies their personal religious needs and has meaning for them. They are devoting more time to meditation, spiritual reflection, and the spiritual needs their humanity requires.

More people are attending religious services more regularly. In Canada, for example, 44% of the people attend Church services every week, and most people attend some religious services on a monthly basis. In the United States, 42% of the people attend religious services every week and another 40% attend "frequently." A very high proportion of teenagers pray regularly, and a good number express great satisfaction with spiritual retreats and religious activities that are "meaningful." They show great interest in religious vocations, and are anxious to be involved with charitable activities that have a religious base.

More and more of the adult population are actively engaged in the religious activities of their particular denomination, support the apostolic and mission endeavors of their Church, and cooperate in interfaith charitable, political, and cultural experiences. One in three adult Christians in the United States and Canada describes himself or herself as a "born again" Christian, 500,000 are members of some charismatic movement, and a majority attempt to make some kind of personal commitment to Christ effective in their lives. The **evangelical** Churches are experiencing unprecedented growth.

Moreover, newspaper, magazine, radio, and TV reports regularly testify to the fact that religiously committed people, both lay and **clerical,** are

satisfying to the human soul. They have even less faith in the political processes that shape their economic, political, and cultural expressions. They are disturbed by the emphasis on sensual gratification that permeates a large segment of the entertainment media. They are unhappy with the lessening of **moral** certitudes and the shirking of personal responsibility for moral decisions.*

---

*See especially Arnold A. Rogow's *The Dying of the Light: A Searching Look at America Today.* (New York: G.P. Putnam & Sons, 1975).

5

actively involved in the political process, and are giving religion and religious values a larger and more effective voice in society. They demonstrate that religion has a dimension to add to society that no other cultural influence has, and that that dimension wishes to be heard and included in political decision-making. Their presence is felt and their voices heard in the fight against crime, corruption, moral decay, and ethical relativism. They are not ashamed to profess their religious beliefs and values in the public forum and are calling for a return to traditional religious values in education, law, politics, and government.

Over and above these particular evidences of the growing influence of religion on the private and public lives of the people of North America, there is a more general influence: most people in Canada, the United States, and Mexico have a positive attitude toward religion. In Canada and the United States religion is generally respected in all levels of society. Its **ministers** are given a special deference, its ceremonies are revered, its major celebrations are observed, and its life-meanings are generally accepted. It is recognized as having a strong, positive influence on North American culture, and its traditions are respected for what they have contributed to North American growth. Above all, in spite of isolated instances of harassment, religion is freely practiced in all the countries making up the North American complex.

It hardly need be asserted that religion is a terribly important loyalty in American society since many previous research publications have established this fact. What we are arguing . . . is that religion is a means of social differentiation, and as a modality of participation in a larger American society it is a manifestation of the fact that America is a denominational society— that is to say, a society in which denominational loyalty profoundly affects much of what a young person learns as he grows up, many of the decisions he will make in his life, and the kinds of relationships he will have with other Americans. It also means that loyalty to the religious tradition, particularly to those doctrinal, ethical, and cultic elements which are of major symbolic importance in the context of American society will be extremely important to the young American for his becoming himself and being an American. Devotional practice and doctrinal orthodoxy have persisted in American society . . . because sociologically and psychologically such attitudes are important to being a member of the American society. . . .

For a wide variety of reasons, it is relatively easy to grow up as a moderately religious person in American society and relatively difficult to be totally irreligious. That is not to say that a young person cannot be raised an **atheist** or become an atheist in his formative years. But religion is so much a part of both the self-definition and the social location of most Americans that the strain and thrust is toward some kind of conscious and explicit religious affiliation.

—Andrew Greeley, *The Denominational Society* (Glenview, Illinois: Scott, Foresman and Company, 1973), pp. 232–235.

The Characteristics of Religion in North America

People in the world express their religion differently, and people within religious groups express their religion differently. The Buddhists, for example, differ in their religious expression from Moslems, and Catholics in Italy differ from Catholics in Africa in the ways they express their Catholicism.

Circumstances of time and place also affect the way people express their religion. It is very difficult, for example, for the people of communist Russia or mainland China to express their religion or their religious feelings openly, but it is very easy for the people in, say, West Germany or the United States to express their religion and their religious feelings. Because, for the most part, the circumstances of history, geography, economics, politics, and culture have been generally favorable to the free development of religious expression, the religions and the religious expressions of the peoples of North America have taken on certain distinguishing characteristics.

Religion in Mexico

Because of its history, religious expression in Mexico is Spanish/ Mexican. It is steeped in Spanish Catholic traditions, tempered by the native Mexican culture which is chiefly Indian/Aztec. Popular religious expression is characterized by fierce

NORTH AMERICA

loyalty, deep and expressive piety, reverence, and respect not unmixed with fear. Official Mexican policy, however, toward established Churches and their ministers has been plainly repressive since the end of the nineteenth century. While open persecution officially ended in the mid-1940s, when more lenient policies were enacted, institutional religions still labor under legal and practical difficulties.

Among the general populace, however, religion is taken as a matter of course, with approximately 93 percent of the population being Roman Catholic. Indeed, because Catholicism and the emergence of the Mexican nation are indissolubly linked in history, traditional pious practices of Catholicism form part of the very fabric of Mexican life and culture.

The Spanish conquistadors, clergy, and colonists who poured into the New World were determined to win Indian souls for Christ and the Church. However, the native religions they attempted to supplant were built upon complex belief systems and long-established practices, which were not totally replaced by Christianity. Many of the early Indian converts held on to the old gods, clothed in Catholic tradition. The influence of the Aztec religion may be seen in Mexican religious practice even today, for example, in the pagan pageantry that informs many local fiestas.

Religion in Canada

Like religion in Mexico, religion in Canada is a product of the history of Canada. First extensively settled by the French and then taken over by the English, Canada has two distinct cultural strains (and two languages): French and English. Religion in Canada reflects the characteristics of both. It is predominantly Roman Catholic in the French-speaking areas of Canada (though there are many English-speaking Roman Catholics in other areas), and predominantly Protestant or "other" in the English-speaking areas.

Canada came under European influence when a French explorer, Samuel de Champlain, established the first permanent settlement in Quebec in 1608, claiming the entire territory for the French king. Canada remained exclusively French until the British Hudson's Bay Company was established in 1670. The French controlled the eastern half of Canada and the Illinois and Louisiana Territories until the English armies, under General Wolfe, captured the principal French military forts in 1758 and 1759. Canada finally came under complete British control at the signing of the Peace of Paris in 1763, which ended the Seven Year's War (the French and Indian War in North America). By the Treaty of Versailles in 1783, Great Britain and the United States established the US/Canada border, which was extended to the Rocky Mountains in 1818. The present border along the 49th parallel was extended to the Pacific in 1846.

It is important to remember that even though, because of its history, Canada is often thought of as "British"—and the French Canadians are often considered "French"—both are fervently Canadian. They think of themselves as neither British nor French, but as Canadian, and specifically as "French Canadian" or "British Canadian."

Religiously, Canadians are not so denominationally diversified nor experiential as the people of the United States are.

However, Canadian Church attendance is about the same as that of the United States (44% to 42% respectively), the religious concerns of the two countries are somewhat parallel, and their support of religion and religious institutions is nearly equal. A major difference between the two is the Canadian attitude toward financial support for religion and religious education. In most Canadian provinces, the government allows financial support to religious schools; in the United States, the government does not.

Religion in the United States

Religion in the United States, like the religious expressions in Mexico and Canada, was shaped by the history, geography, economics, politics, and culture of the country as it grew from a colonial and missionary status to a world power. At first there were three separate "religious regions" in the U.S.: the southwest was Catholic Christian—the Indians being brought into the Christian culture of the Spanish missionaries; the midwest was under the influence of French Catholic missionaries; and the northeast was predominantly English and Dutch Protestant. Later, the south formed a fourth region which became almost exclusively Baptist.

As time went on, immigrants came to the United States from all over Europe, and the western expansion took place. The United States became a pluralistic society with many expressions of Christianity. Pockets of religious expressions, or denominations, developed in various parts of the United States, and, because of the religious hostilities generated in Europe, these denominations remained more or less isolated from each other, living in a kind of uneasy truce. Finally, religion in the United States developed its own characteristics, described by sociologist Andrew Greeley as activist, **pragmatic,** American, pluralistic, independent, individualistic, experimental, and open. Lately, religion in the United States has been experiencing an evangelistic renewal, with an emphasis on converting people to live strictly by the gospel.

Perhaps the single most distinctive characteristic of the religious movement in the United States, however, is its openness to experimentation. Literally hundreds of religious groups have sprung up in the United States which express their religious understanding in a variety of ways. These groups range from those who practice witchcraft, voodoo, black **magic,** and the like, to "other century" religious expressions such as the **Mennonites** and the **Amish,** or modern movements such as the Hari Krishna, the "Jesus people," and the "Moonies." All have found a place somewhere in American society.

The American Religion

The historical, geographical, political, and social realities of the United States and Canada have added a dimension

to the present state of religion in the United States and Canada which is not found in most other areas of the world. That dimension has variously been called "The American Religion," "The Civil Religion," or "The American Way of Life."

This "American Religion" is not a religion in the traditional understanding of the term. It has no Church, no religious or institutional structure, no formal theology, and no set form of worship. It does, however, have (as formal religions have), a religious faith, a code of ethical behavior, a way of looking at reality, and a set of basic values that enable us to call it a religion, and a way to identify it as a kind of religion.

If it is not a religion in its formal sense, what is this "American Religion"? It is a way of life shared by most religious peoples in the United States and Canada, based on belief in God and a way of life, and rooted in general commitment to religious principles and practices that transcend the beliefs and practices of any particular denominational group. It has a common religious sense, contains generally accepted ethical principles, and subscribes to common religious values participated in by all the major religious groups, to form a kind of super national religion that is peculiarly North American.

It should be clear that what is being designated under [the American Religion] is not the so-called "common denominator" religion; it is not a synthetic system composed of beliefs to be found in all or in a group of religions. It is an organic structure of ideas, values, and beliefs that constitutes a faith common

11

to all Americans and genuinely operative in their lives, a faith that markedly influences, and is influenced by, the 'official' religions of American society. . . . It is the characteristic American religion, undergirding American life and overreaching American society despite all indubitable differences of region, section, culture and class.

—Will Herberg, *Protestant, Catholic, Jew,* (Garden City, New York: Doubleday, 1955), p. 77.

This "American Religion" grew out of the necessities imposed by the history, geography, political process, and social situation in the United States and Canada. The nature of the immigration patterns to the New World, the vastness of the area to be settled—as well as its topography, democratic system of government, and divergent cultural expressions of the immigrants—all these factors worked together to prevent any single religious group from imposing its faith or religious practices in the United States and Canada. The various religious groups learned to live together and to accommodate themselves to the political and social realities of the new order.

Out of this emerged another kind of religious expression—an expression in which traditional religious groups could express their own religion in a new, "American" way.

The Humanist Influence on North American Religion

If religion and religious expression in North America has been influenced by what we have called the American religion, it is almost equally influenced by what is known as "**humanism.**"

Humanism is a way of looking at life and human experience from a people-centered perspective rather than from a God-centered perspective. Its primary concerns are humanity and the meaning of human experience, the dignity of the human person, the rights of human beings as human beings, and the worth of human life as it is lived on earth. Humanists look to human interests, values, and concerns in their search for the meaning of life, rather than to supernatural interests, values, and concerns exclusively. They are more concerned with the quality of life lived here on earth than they are with the promise of salvation in the next.

Some humanists, it is true, look to the human mind and to human experience alone for moral and spiritual guidance, and some reject altogether the idea of a God, of revelation, and of supernatural help or power affecting human affairs, but, by and large, humanists do not dismiss the idea of a God, **revelation,** or divine assistance. They simply put their emphasis on the inherent dignity of human beings as human beings, and they believe that human beings have a nature and destiny that are important in themselves. For humanists, people come first; everything else follows.

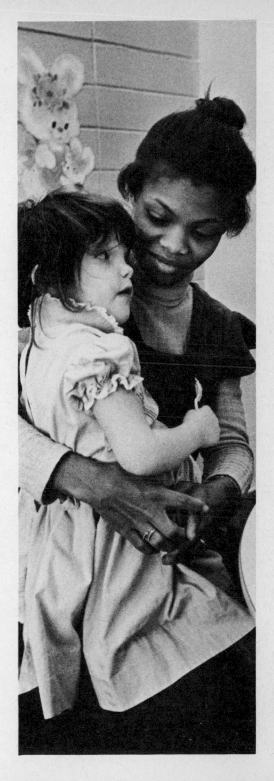

Among other things, humanism has been a factor in making North American religions, generally, more human, and has affected the institutional religions directly and indirectly. It has caused most of them to rethink their orientation and to reorder their priorities, and to pay more attention to the realities of human experience than most institutional religions did in the past. Humanism has also helped most North American institutional religions to temper their approaches to such things as **salvation,** sin, forgiveness, judgment, and the punishment of God. It has helped to influence most of them to recast their theology concerning the relationship between God and people and between people and the institutional Church. It has helped most of them to become more ecumenical and to take a world-view rather than a sectarian view. In some few cases, it has affected doctrinal stances in a radical way, but, for the most part, humanism has helped to lead the institutional religions to pay more attention to the concerns of this world and to the religious needs of people as they live out their lives.

Other Religious Expressions and Experiences Affecting Religion in North America

In addition to the "American Religion" and Humanist effects on

religions and religious expressions in North America, there are other religious expressions and experiences affecting the general tenor of religion in North America. Among the most significant are the pentecostal, **charismatic,** and **cult** movements, the reporting of religious and mystical experiences, and the "experiences of dying" documentations of Dr. Elisabeth Kubler-Ross, Dr. Raymond A. Moody, and others. These movements and experiences are not religions as such; they are movements within, and often outside of, established religions.

Pentecostalism* sprang up among Protestant groups in the United States before the Revolutionary War. It was characterized by dynamic, and sometimes frightening, preaching about the sinfulness of people, God's wrath and stern judgment, the probability of eternal damnation, the evils visited on sinful people by an angry God, and the necessity of being "saved"; by religious meetings designed to provoke spiritual frenzy; by an insistence on rigid adherence to Biblical literalism; and by a pledge to renounce Satan and the sinful works of "the world." It affected the tenor of Protestantism in the eastern and southern parts of the United States until well into the twentieth century. It survives today in isolated areas of the United States and Canada.

The modern pentecostal movement—or, as it is more often called "The Charismatic Movement"—is not to be confused with old-line pentecostalism. It is characterized by

---

*Not to be confused with what are known as Pentecostal Assemblies or Assemblies of God, which are established religious groups.

what its adherents call "a second baptism." This second baptism is "baptism in the Spirit" which those who have experienced it say is a real experiencing of the coming of the Holy Spirit into their lives.

Modern pentecostals,* or charismatics, come from all Christian denominations and include people of all social classes. There are well over three million charismatics in the United States and Canada (there are no figures for Mexico), and a goodly number of them are ministers, priests, and Protestant and Catholic religious.** They seem to have these things in common:

(1) a conviction of their baptism "in the Spirit";
(2) a search for a deeper spiritual life;
(3) an intense devotion to Jesus Christ;
(4) an acceptance of the Christian scriptures as God's direct word to each charismatic;
(5) an acceptance of the charismatic gifts (hence, the name "charismatics");†
(6) spiritual joy displayed in the private lives and community gatherings of charismatics;
(7) spiritual peace and confidence in God;
(8) an increased prayer life;
(9) an **evangelical** spirit—the urging of others to experience the Spirit.

"The phenomena of pentecostal, charismatic, or **glossolaliacal** experiences are, of course, nothing new," says Leo Rosten in his *Religions*

*Modern Pentecostalism gets its name from the urging of the leaders of the movement for people to listen to the Holy Spirit, and be like the Christians who received the Holy Spirit at the first **Pentecost.**

**Those who belong to a monastic or religious order.

†The **charisms,** Christians believe, are divinely conferred gifts, or powers, upon individuals for the good of the community or the spread of the Christian message. They are never considered as rewards, or signs of God's favor to an individual. These charisms, Christians believe, are speaking in tongues, the gift of prophecy, the interpretation of tongues, faith, wisdom, knowledge of divine things, the power of healing, the recognition of spirits, and the performing of miracles. (**See:** The First Epistle of Paul to the Corinthians 12:8–10)

of America, [page 592]. " 'The old time religion,' healing by 'laying on hands,' miraculous cures, outburst of prophecy, ecstatic testimonies to being born or reborn or truly baptized by being possessed by the Spirit—these are familiar phenomena in American history. . . . Part of the appeal of the new 'charisma' groups is the liberating sense of **ecumenism;** for the first time, Protestants and Catholics (including priests and **nuns**), ministers and laymen, evangelists and conservative Church-goers, pray together, sing together, embrace, heal by the 'laying on of hands,' and share in self- and group-induced seizures of spiritual **ecstasy.**"

The history of the Pentecostal Movements is significant. It reveals men's unconscious desire for spiritual nourishment in this twentieth century as a counter to the anguish which they feel at the Age de la mort de Dieu. It is not only the Assemblies of God, but all sects, all Churches of recent origin that are asking the Established Churches a searching question. If men and women of goodwill, who cannot all be crazy or weak in the head, turn to religious groups with such diverse doctrines, it is obviously because in the Established Churches they do not find what they are seeking. [They] seem to be a form of historical judgment pronounced on the older Churches. . . . [These movements] spring from a true spirituality. The religion which is preached is founded on piety, personal experience of God, search for direct contact with Him and the necessity of bearing witness in public to the supernatural realities

which each adherent has experienced. Much of the success depends on the degree of enthusiasm, fervour and joy engendered; their aim, . . . 'is to touch your heart, not fill your head.' This means an excessive appeal to sentiment, . . . but they have merit in that they oppose routine, conformism and pharisaism, and that they sometimes arouse that 'inner warmth' which the disciples at Emmaus felt when the resurrected Jesus spoke to them. . . .

This appeal to sentiment stands out in fact as a warm humanity

which, it must be said, is not the main characteristic of the Haute Societe protestante in their Reformed Churches, nor of the vast Catholic parishes of our great cities.

—*Our Brothers in Christ,* by Henri Daniel-Rops. (New York: E.P. Dutton & Company, 1967), page 58.

The Jesus Movement, as it is called, includes a diverse number of religious people who have "turned to Christ" in a variety of ways. Among the more prominent groups are the "born again Christians," the "Youth for Christ," the "Fellowship of Christian Athletes," and the "Jesus People."

Like the charismatics, those involved in the Jesus movement are interdenominational, but unlike the charismatics, the Jesus movement includes many who belong to no religious group. It also includes a small number of Jewish youths who call themselves "Jews for Jesus," and, marginally, such groups as the "Christian Surfers," the "I am" group, and a host of others who proclaim their belief in the attachment to Jesus in slogans, signs, symbols, rituals,

encounters of one kind or another, meetings, songfests, rock concerts, all night vigils, sunrise services, and the like.

The "born again Christians" are those fifty million Christians who, having experienced a "new conversion," commit themselves to Jesus Christ totally in a public confession of faith.* They speak of themselves as having been born again because, they say, they have experienced Christ in a real and

Gallup Opinion Index for 1977–78.

dramatic way and have turned their lives over to him without reservation. In so doing, they say, they feel born again and feel committed not only to the principles of Christ, but also to the person of Christ as their personal savior, to whom they promise complete and absolute allegiance. Like the charismatics, the "born again Christians" say that they experience an inner peace, a renewed spiritual life, complete confidence in Christ as savior, and God speaking to them directly in the Christian Bible.

The Pentecostals, the Charismatics, the born again Christians, and the Jesus People have had a profound influence on religion and the religious atmosphere in the United States and Canada. They have made certain forms of religious expression acceptable in even sophisticated circles and have made the public manifestation of religious fervor respectable everywhere. They have also contributed greatly to what we have called "The American Religion" by helping organized religion shed some of its strictly denominational biases, and have contributed to the role of religion as a factor in the public forum. They have played a major role in increasing the influence that religion has on North American life.

A phenomenon of religious expression in the United States, will spill-over effects in Canada and the border areas of Mexico, is the perennial emergence of religious and pseudo-religious cult groups. These cults attract, for the most part, white, upper and middle class college-age North Americans who, disillusioned with—or unsatisfied by—life as they experience it, search for answers to the problems of living by withdrawing from the life activities and experiences of their peer group. They join these cults, submit themselves to a strict lifestyle, and engage in religious or mystical experiences designed to bring them the peace, satisfaction, purpose, and security for which they long. These cults exist outside of the mainstream of the religious and cultural life of North America and have only a marginal effect on religion and culture.*

Extraordinary Religious Experiences

According to the *Gallup Opinion Index for 1977-78,* nearly 31% of adult Americans have experienced a unique, sudden, and dramatic religious insight or awakening. The people who have had these special religious experiences are from all social classes, all religions, all educational levels, and all ages.

As more and more becomes known of these experiences, more and more people are reporting them as having happened to them specifically. Of those who say they have had such an experience, 10% report an "other-worldly" feeling of union with a Divine Being; 5% report a spiritual awakening related to nature; 5% report an experience related to healing; 4% report experiencing visions, voices, and dreams of a spiritual nature; and 2% report a sudden insight and turning to God in a moment of severe crisis like death or near-death. All report that their

experience has had a profound effect on their lives, and has caused them to turn more to God, to prayer, to the concerns of the spirit, and to helping other people, especially those in difficulty.

- *"I was reading the Bible one night and couldn't sleep. A vision appeared to me. It was frozen and motionless. I saw an unusual light that wasn't there—but it was. There was a great awareness of someone else being in that room with me."*
- *"I was having a lot of marital problems and was really discouraged with life. Then suddenly I experienced a closeness with God and this has changed my life and my attitudes."*
- *"I felt a surge of inspiration and reawakening at the time of my wife's death."*
- *"My little boy was hit by a car and critically injured. The doctors said he was dying. But I prayed to God for his life and I felt in my entire being a joyous sensation. I knew then that he would be spared, and God answered my prayers."*

—*Gallup Opinion Index 1977-78,* "Religion in America," (Princeton, New Jersey: The American Institute of Public Opinion) page 55.

Closely related to these unique religious experiences are the "experiences of dying" phenomena that have been reported in the last few years. These reports deal with what people who have been resuscitated after having been pronounced clinically dead said about their experience of dying; with what people who have

---

*See pages 191-2 for a description of some of these cults.

come very close to death in accidents or after severe injury have said; and with reports of other persons who have reported either an experience they have had with someone else's death, or who have reported hearing, firsthand, the experience of dying that was told to them by someone else who had had such an experience. In each case, the person "dead" or very close to dying had experienced a phenomenon dealing with the passage from life as it is experienced in the usual way to a stage of life beyond the three-dimensional life all human beings experience on earth.

I became very seriously ill, and the doctor put me in the hospital. This one morning a solid gray mist gathered around me, and I left my body. I had a floating sensation as I felt myself get out of my body,

and I looked back and I could see myself on the bed below and there was no fear. It was quiet—very peaceful and serene. I was not in the least bit upset or frightened. It was just a tranquil feeling, and it was something which I didn't dread. I felt that maybe I was dying, and I felt that if I did not get back to my body, I would be dead, gone.
—Raymond A. Moody, Jr., M.D. *Life After Life.* (New York: Bantam Books, 1976), page 38.

This experience took place during the birth of my first child. About the eighth month of my pregnancy, I developed what my doctor described as a toxic condition and advised me to enter the hospital where he could force labor. It was immediately after delivery that I had a severe hemorrhage and the

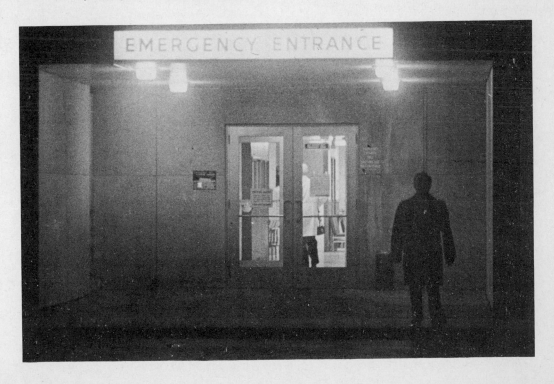

doctor had a difficult time controlling it. I was aware of what was happening as, having been a nurse myself, I realized the danger. At this time, I lost consciousness, and heard an annoying buzzing, ringing sound. The next thing I knew it seemed as if I were on a ship or a small vessel sailing to the other side of a large body of water. On the distant shore, I could see all of my loved ones who had died—my mother, my father, my sister, and others. I could see them, could see their faces, just as they were when I knew them on earth. They seemed to be beckoning me to come on over, and all the while I was saying, "No, no, I'm not ready to join you. I don't want to die. I'm not ready to go."

Now, this was the strangest experience because all this time I could see all the doctors and nurses, too, as they worked on my body, but it seemed as if I were a spectator rather than that person—that body—they were working on. I was trying so hard to get through to my doctor, "I'm not going to die," but no one could hear me. Everything—the doctors, the nurses, the delivery room, the ship, the water, and the far shore—was just sort of a conglomerate. It was all together, as if one scene were superimposed right on top of the other.

Finally, the ship almost reached the far shore, but just before it did, it turned around and started back. I did finally get through to my doctor, and I was saying, "I'm not going to die." It was at this point, I guess, that I came around, and the doctor explained what had happened, that

I had had a post-partum hemorrhage, and that they had nearly lost me, but that I was going to be all right.
—*Ibid.*, pp. 74-75

The reports of these experiences have become more widespread in the past few years, because research in this area of human experience has increased. In former years, people who had such experiences often either kept them to themselves lest they be considered deranged, or have told them only to trusted confidants.

I was pretty popular in junior high and high school, and I just floated with the crowd, never anything new. I was a follower, not a leader. And after this happened to

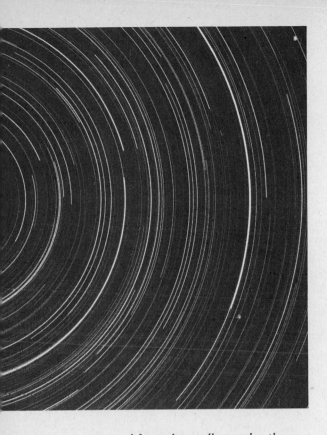

levels, and all religious and non-religious persuasions, include certain common denominators: "inexpressible" (that is, the experience defies explanation—it cannot be described exactly); feelings of peace and quiet; a "dark tunnel"; being outside of the body; meeting other spiritual beings or "a being of light"; approaching a border or limit; and the experience of "coming back."

Most persons who have had this experience of dying, of course, have had other feelings or experiences also, but these particular experiences are not common to all of them. What is common is the feelings of the absolute reality of the experience and its importance to the person himself. There is absolutely no doubt in the minds of all who have reported on this experience of dying that something extraordinary happened to them and that there is "something" beyond earthly life as it is experienced and that that something is a dimension of existence that is above and infinitely better than life on earth as they experienced it.

me, and I tried to tell people, they just automatically labeled me as crazy, I think. I would try to tell people this, and they would listen with interest, but then I would find out later that they'd go say, "She has really flipped out." When I saw that it was just a big joke, I quit trying to communicate about it. I hadn't been trying to get across the idea that, "Gee, this strange experience has happened to me." What I was trying to say was that there was more we needed to know about life than I had ever thought about, and I am sure they hadn't, either.
—*Ibid.*, p. 86

The reports, from people of all ages, all social backgrounds, all educational

I was hospitalized for a severe kidney condition, and I was in a coma for approximately a week. My doctors were extremely uncertain as to whether I would live. During this period when I was unconscious, I felt as though I were lifted right up, just as though I didn't have a physical body at all. A brilliant white light appeared to me. The light was so bright that I could not see through it, but going into its presence was so calming and so wonderful. There is just no experience on earth like it. In the presence of the light, the thoughts or

words came into my mind: "Do you want to die?" And I replied that I didn't know since I knew nothing about death. Then the white light said, "Come over this line and you will learn." I felt that I knew where the line was in front of me although I could not actually see it. As I went across the line, the most wonderful feelings came over me—fellings of peace, tranquility, a vanishing of all worries.
　—*Ibid.,* p. 75.

There was a feeling of utter peace and quiet, no fear at all, and I found myself in a tunnel—a tunnel of concentric circles. Shortly after that, I saw a T.V. program called The Time Tunnel, *where people go back in time through this spiralling tunnel. Well, that's the closest thing to it that I can think of.*
　—*Ibid.,* p. 33.

I had the feeling that I was moving through a deep, very dark valley. The darkness was so deep and impenetrable that I could see absolutely nothing but this was the most wonderful, worry-free experience you can imagine.
　—*Ibid.*

These reports have not affected the persons who have experienced the phenomena alone; they have affected all who have studied them and all who have heard of them. Some have greeted them with skepticism; others have listened to them thoughtfully and learned from them. Religion, religious people, and religious institutions have been affected by them because they can no longer deal with one of life's profoundest mysteries—death—without taking them into consideration.

Conclusion

From what you have read and discussed in this chapter, you can see that religion in North America is very much alive. It plays a significant role in the way most people live their lives, raise their children, relate to each other, and govern themselves. While the expression of religion in North America is largely denominational, it is also, in a different and significant way, non-sectarian. It has served, and continues to serve, as an important underpinning for the economic, political, social, and cultural expression of the peoples of North America.

To appreciate the role of religion in North America, it is necessary to look at the various religious expressions that have been, and are, operative in Canada, the United States, and Mexico. The most prominent, of course, is Christianity in its **Protestant** and Catholic expressions. Playing lesser, but nonetheless significant, roles in the development of North American religious culture are the Jewish, the **Eastern Orthodox,** the "American born" religions, like the Church of Jesus Christ of the Latter day Saints (**Mormons**) and the many smaller religious groups not associated with the larger groups, such as the Unitarians.

But before any of these can be discussed, the religion of the earliest Americans—the Indians, the Eskimos, the Aleuts, and the Hawaiians—must be considered. They, too, are part of the story of religion in North America.

For Review and Discussion

1. What reasons does your book give for saying that religion in North America is still a force in shaping North American culture?
2. Discuss whether or not religion plays a role in shaping the culture of teenagers in the North America.
3. Why do religious expressions differ in various parts of the world? What experiences have you had that might confirm this fact?
4. What are the general characteristics of religion in Mexico? Are these generally true for other North Americans of Latino background?
5. What historical factors shaped religious expression in Canada?
6. What "religious regions" existed in the United States in its early history?
7. What are some of the general characteristics of religious expression in the United States? Explain.
8. What is meant by "the American Religion"? Do you think it is a good thing? Why or why not?
9. Discuss whether or not religion should effect the economic, political, and social life of a country.
10. What influence have "charismatic Christians," "born again" Christians, and the Jesus People had on religion in North America? If you have had any experience with these movements, describe your reactions.
11. Discuss what possible dangers might be present in various kinds of religious expression.
12. Be sure you can define the following words:

atheist	evangelical
charism	humanist
charismatic	mystical
clerical	pentecostal
cult	pragmatic
denomination	religious pluralism
ecstasy	transcend
ecumenicism	

For Research

1. In newspapers, magazines, or TV presentations, find examples of current religious activities which are affecting the economic, political, or social life of North America.
2. Prepare a short report on religious activities or experiences in your area.
3. Find out what a Church group in your area is doing to influence political, social, or economic life.
4. Find out what you can about the voices heard by Joan of Arc. In what way are these voices related to material in this chapter?

2

The Religion of the Earliest Americans

TABOO
maya
totem
AZTEC ·
· ojibway
POLYNESIAN
sioux sun · ALASKA CHEYENNE · manitou ·
RITE

Many people think the history of North America began when Christopher Columbus "discovered" America in 1492. Actually, the history of North America—as far as people are concerned—is now believed to have begun some 30,000 years ago when the first human beings crossed over what is now called the Bering Straits from Siberia to Alaska.

These forebears of the race mistakenly called "Indian" by Columbus (who thought he had reached East India taking a westerly route from Spain) came, it now seems likely, from northeast Asia, commonly called Siberia. These earliest Americans probably found their way to continental North America when the **"Beringia Bridge"** (the land under the Bering Straits) was exposed due to the formation of gigantic inland ice sheets from the waters covering the Bering Straits, during the **Ice Age** that occurred between 30,000 and 36,000 years ago. As time went on, they probably found their way south along a corridor between the eastern slopes of the Rocky Mountains and the Dakota

Plains. This migration took many hundreds of years, and was dictated by the necessity of finding food and escaping the press of severe winters and massive ice sheets (there was another Ice Age between 13,000 and 20,000 years ago).

Over the next several centuries, these people migrated south toward New Mexico and Central America, and east and southeast toward New York and Florida, populating the entire North American land mass from the timberline in Canada to Panama. Some of them eventually migrated along the western coast of South America as far south as Tierra del Fuego, the southernmost point of Chile, and east to the Atlantic shores of South America. Scientists now believe that this entire process—the migrations and the populating of the Americas—took some 25,000 years, and included various groups of these "Indians" of differing physical types.

If you recall the vast changes that have taken place in, for example, the United States since the first settlers landed at Plymouth Rock in 1620 A.D., it is easy to see what changes must have taken place among the people in North America in the 25,000 years after their first coming to this Western Hemisphere. They not only populated both continents, but they eventually also settled in particular geographical areas and developed separate cultures, separating into **tribes,** or kinship groups, that were as distinct from each other as the Canadian English, The American English, Australian English, and British English are from one another. Some of these tribes developed cultures that rival the more

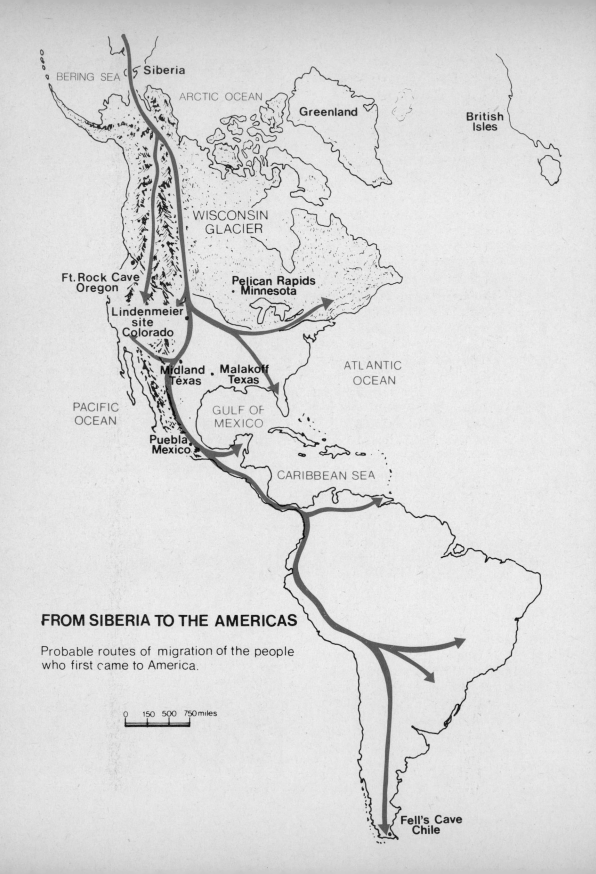

BERING SEA
Siberia
ARCTIC OCEAN
Greenland
British
Isles

WISCONSIN
GLACIER

Ft. Rock Cave
Oregon

Pelican Rapids
Minnesota

Lindenmeier
site
Colorado

ATLANTIC
OCEAN

Midland
Texas
Malakoff
Texas

PACIFIC
OCEAN

GULF OF
MEXICO

Puebla
Mexico

CARIBBEAN SEA

FROM SIBERIA TO THE AMERICAS

Probable routes of migration of the people
who first came to America.

0   150   500   750 miles

Fell's Cave
Chile

famous cultures of Greece, Rome, Egypt, and China, which flourished at about the same time.

These earliest Americans were followed by the ancestors of the modern Eskimos* and Aleuts (A-loots) who came across the Bering Straits from Mongolia, settling permanently in Alaska and the Aleutian Islands some 2,500 years ago.** They adapted to the demands of the harsh climate and spread across the entire Alaskan/Canadian glacier areas, preserving their culture and their ways almost unchanged until well into the twentieth century. Unlike those who preceded them, they never attempted to migrate to warmer climates.

The third group of earliest Americans, the Hawaiians, came to the Hawaiian Islands over 1000 years ago from the Marquesas Islands some 2000 miles to the southeast of Hawaii, and from Tahiti and the Society Islands 2,200 miles to the south of Hawaii about 800 years ago. Both groups came across this vast expanse of the Pacific Ocean in open boats, a feat unsurpassed in the history of navigation. Their descendants form a distinct minority among the 800,000 people who now live in the Hawaiian Islands, and the "pure" Hawaiians are having a difficult time preserving even the vestiges of their **Polynesian** culture.

---

*The word *Eskimo* comes from the Algonquin word *Eskamantik* meaning "eater of raw flesh."

**The word *Alaska* comes from the Aleut word meaning "Great Land." The Eskimos and the Aleuts are not from the same racial stock as the original Indians of North America.

Religion of the Earliest Americans

Religion played an important role in the lives of the earliest Americans. The existence of spirits, powers, forces, or gods in the world was an accepted fact for all of these people, and their lives were attuned to the rhythms of their world as it was controlled by these spirits or gods.

The earliest Americans, for the most part, practiced some form or another of **animism.** Animism is a belief that all beings, natural objects (including all animals and even trees), natural phenomena, and nature itself possess souls or spirits that must be reckoned with before any activity could be undertaken. A particular spirit, or spirits, had to be recognized, addressed, dealt with, outdone, offset, or cooperated with to insure success in any undertaking.

Religion and law were one [in Hawaii] and above all were four great gods. Kane, the supremacy, was represented by the sun. Others were Lono, of fruitful earth; Ku, of power and force; and Kanaloa of the sea. All were males. Beneath them were dozens of lesser gods, some female: Pele of volcanoes, Hina of the moon, and Laka of dance. These are but a few. There were many thousands of other gods—of different rains, winds, cliffs, lagoons, mountains and valleys. A fishpond acquired its own sacred spirit.

There were gods under gods under gods. Craftsmen, farmers,

Hawaiian War god. Peabody Museum of Salem. Photo by M.W. Sexton.

seers, midwives and meteorologists had occupational gods called akua. Tens of thousands of fishermen had their own gods, the kuula, enshrined in seashore altars. Lowliest, yet most personal of all, were the aumakua of a family. Some were carved in rude figures. Many were simple pieces of unworked coral or stone. Daily offerings of food and water were made and prayers chanted, not to the earth-scraps of the aumakua, but to their living power and protection.

Of the humans, only the alii, the high chiefs, conversed with the greater gods and communicated their benevolence—or rage. As descendants of the gods, this was their birthright. And through them the gods ruled.

This was the heathen, before the white man came.

—Reprinted with permission from *The Hawaiians.* © 1970 by Island Heritage Ltd.

Religious Practices

Although most early Americans believed in a "Great Spirit," or principal God, in every case they developed elaborate **rituals,** prayers, ceremonies, magical rites, acts of worship, sacrifices, offerings, tribal dances, incantations, invocations, **taboos,** and **totemic** symbols, with appropriate headdress, body paint, **amulets,** masks, and capes, to accompany each **rite** for a particular spirit which they believed inhabited a particular place or thing, or controlled a particular activity. Each rite or ceremony was designed to express a

particular relationship with a particular spirit, to secure the favor or assistance of a friendly spirit, or to ward off the hostility of an evil spirit.

Aware of the blessings nature lavished on them, the Northwest Indians developed spiritual practices to ensure continued riches. Animals, the Indians held, lived expressly to nourish man; yet every animal possessed an immortal, willful spirit that could interrupt the supply of riches and bring sickness or death. Hence, religious practice often took ths form of honoring, flattering and generally keeping in the good graces of the animal kingdom.

Whale hunters established spiritual contact with their prey by a regimen of baths, incantations, fasting, sexual abstinence and contemplation in a special shrine. Salmon fishermen, too, felt obliged to woo the fish. When the salmon began their spawning runs, it was thought that they were sacrificing themselves for the benefit of man. As thanks for this act, the first catch was regaled with laudatory speeches and treated like a guest at a potlatch. The bones of subsequent catches, once stripped clean of flesh, were returned to the sea, where, it was believed, they rematerialized as fish.

—Robert Claiborne, *The First Americans,* [The Emergence of Man Series] (New York: Time-Life Books, 1973), page 82.

All activities were ringed with taboos. Illness, misfortune, lack of game, were certainly caused by some broken law that had thrown the world out of balance. A shaman would find out what had gone wrong and correct it. Had the sick woman's husband perhaps speared a salmon at a time when he was restricted? Then of course, the salmon were indignant and would not let themselves be caught. Or perhaps a sin had floated down to the bottom of the sea, to fall like dirt in the hair of the great goddess known as "She Down There." Then of course she was indignant and was keeping the fat creatures of the sea out of reach of those on land, and the shaman would have to make a spirit journey down to her and square things. The shaman, common among many Indians as well as among Siberians, was particularly popular among the Eskimos. Shamans could be women as well as men, maybe better. They performed magic, secured revenge, cured illness, sometimes by a method very widely known among the peoples of both North and South America—sucking out the illness and spitting forth a pebble or some such object to prove it.

—Reprinted by permission from *The American Heritage Book of Indians,* by William Brandon © 1961 by American Heritage Publishing Company, Inc.

The kind of spirit, soul, or power was determined by the being, natural object, or phenomenon itself, and the being, object, or phenomenon was

Soapstone figure. Eskimo fishing. Josephine, Eastern Eskimo, Labrador. Peabody Museum of Salem. Photo by M.W. Sexton.

Soapstone figure. Eskimo killing seal. *Eliza, Eastern Eskimo, Labrador. Peabody Museum of Salem. Photo by M.W. Sexton.*

directly related to the environment or the need of the tribe or group practicing a particular form of animism. The Eskimo, for example, practiced rituals or forms of magic associated with the powers or spirits of the extremely cold Alaskan environment, asking for help in the hunt for food: whales, sea elephants, fish, and the small game that roamed the Arctic. The Indians of the eastern part of the United States and Canada developed rituals and practices related to the powers or spirits they believed inhabited the forests, lakes, streams, mountains, and valleys of the eastern part of North America. The Indians of the southwestern part of the United States and the northwestern part of Mexico practiced a religion designed to deal with the spirits or gods of the desert. The Hawaiians, because their lives were bound up with the sea and the "endless June days," practiced a religion whose principal forces or spirits lived in the ocean, the islands, the endless skies, and the tranquil weather.

The Religion
of the
Ojebway Indians*

The various tribes of the Ojebway nation scattered along the shores of the great lakes universally believe in the existence of one Supreme Being; whom they call *Keche-munedoo*, which literally signifies *the Great Spirit*, or Kezha-munedoo, the Benevolent or Merciful Spirit. Believing Him to abound in love and mercy towards his creatures, they suppose him too exalted to concern Himself with the follies of poor earthly beings, whose existence lasts only as it were for a day, his chief care being that of supplying their daily wants. *Munedoo* [or manitou] means a spirit, either good or bad. In order to designate the character or nature of the spirit, they use the prefixes, as in the words above-mentioned.

They also believe in the existence of an evil spirit, whom they call *Mahje-munedoo*. This spirit, they imagine, possesses power to injure any who dare to offend him; and, in order to retain his friendship and appease his anger, some have been known to offer sacrifice to him, so that he might not bring upon them death, illness, or bad luck in hunting.

They, moreover, believe that there are innumerable subordinate deities, or spirits, who have particular control over the affairs of this world. For instance, they believe that there is one god who has the charge of *game,* another who presides over the *fish* and the water, another who controls the winds and the storms, and another who watches over the vegetable world.

These imaginary deities become the objects of their invocations when they are so circumstanced as to require their blessing. For instance, if an Indian wishes for success on a hunting excursion, he will direct his offering and prayer to the god who presides over the deer, the bear, or the beaver, (a wonderful gamekeeper he must be,) that success may attend him; or, if he desires to catch many fish, or have a prosperous voyage, he will sacrifice to the god of the waters. I have known an Indian kill a black dog and throw it into the lake, that he might meet with no disaster whilst on his voyage. In this way the poor dark-minded Indian ignorantly worships the creatures of his own imagination.

The sun, moon, and stars are also adored as gods. At the rising of the sun the old chiefs and warriors chant their hymns of praise to welcome his return; and, at his going down they thank him for the blessing of light and heat during the day. When a visible eclipse of the sun takes place, the poor Indians are thrown into the greatest alarm. They call it the sun's dying, and suppose that he actually dies. In order to assist in bringing him to life again, they stick coals of fire upon the points of their arrows, and shoot them upwards into the air, that by these means the expiring sun may be re-animated and rekindled. The moon and stars are reverenced for the light they give by night, enabling the lonely wanderer to travel in the absence of the sun. . . .

—Rev. Peter Jones, *History of the Ojebway Indians with Especial Reference to their Conversion to Christianity* (London: Houlston and Wright, 1861) pp. 83-84.

*The Ojebway (or Ojibway) Indians lived in Canada and the northern part of the United States around Lake Superior.

Religious Leaders

Every Indian group in North America had its religious specialist—a medicine man, priest, or **shaman**—and most had special places of worship, some of which were architectural monuments lasting into the present century. The medicine man, or shaman, it was believed, had a special relationship with the tribal spirits, could communicate with them, and, in some cases, could control them with magical potions, words, or actions.

Shamans led prayers of the tribe, officiated at tribal religious ceremonies, and often dictated the rules and established the taboos by which the tribe lived. They presided at weddings, conducted the **puberty rites,** attended the sick and the dying, performed sacrifices, conducted elaborate magical rites made prophecies, and counselled the leader of the tribe in all actions dealing with the good or the safety of the tribe. Because of their supposed special relationship with the spirit world, they had a special and sacred status in the tribe. They were sometimes feared but they were always treated with special respect and awe because they were considered holy, wise, and powerful.

Yet Cahokia's** most striking feature was not its protecting palisade or its market and spacious plazas, but the many mounds, large and small, that rose above the city.

A large, well-developed **Amerindian Mound Builder city, which flourished in southern Illinois about 1100 A.D. It dominated an area approximately the size of New York State.

Amerindian shaman

Some of the smaller ones held storehouses for corn and other crops, while larger mounds served as platforms for the houses of the city's more important citizens. For these upper-class Cahokians, a house that was elevated on a mound was a much coveted status symbol.

The biggest, most impressive mounds served less mundane purposes. One of them, a truncated pyramid not far from the city's southwestern entrance, was the location of sacrifices and other religious rituals; a conical mound looming beside it sheltered the graves of the city's illustrious dead.

Dwarfing all was the great steepsided mound that was Cahokia's religious and political center. More than 1,000 feet long—almost four modern city blocks—and nearly 800 feet wide, it rose in several enormous steps. On its topmost level, 100 feet above the city, was a post-and-wattle temple with a sharply peaked roof of thatch. From this vantage point the high priest of Cahokia could keep an eye on another structure beyond the city wall but also under his jurisdiction—an immense circle of posts, more than 100 yards across, which the priesthood used as a combined calendar and solar observatory. Here, seated on a single post set near the circle's center, a priest kept track of the shifting seasons. By noting the position of the sun relative to the surrounding posts as it rose over the bluffs half a mile east of the city, he determined the most propitious time for Cahokian farmers to plant their crops.

—The First Americans, p. 140.

The priest, in addition to his other religious duties, serves as Sun Priest of the village — a position of great prestige and responsibility, since it is he who must determine when crops are to be planted. In this country of high tablelands — the village is more than 6,000 feet above sea level — [in New Mexico's Chaco River Valley] — spring frosts are common, and if the fields are sown too soon the crop will be lost. It is the Sun Priest who, by carefully observing the increasing elevation of the sun at midday, determines when the planting season has arrived.

—Ibid., p. 124.

The Classic Age [300 A.D. *to 1000* A.D.*] in central Mexico was in many respects uncultivated and immature compared to the same period in the realm of the Mayas,* but its works made up in dimension what they lacked in elegance. From the Temple of the Moon to the Temple of Quetzalcoatl, Teotihuacan (Tay-oh-tee-wah-kon), the chief city of the Valley of Mexico's Classic Age, was a solid procession of majestic public buildings and religious barracks, decorated with the serpents, beasts, and feathered men of heaven, dominated in the center by the tremendous Pyramid of the Sun. A paved area more than 3 miles long and nearly 2 miles wide was occupied by these structures and their plazas, parks, and avenues.*

This was less a city than a ceremonial center in the Maya sense.

Long-continued drought in the time of the Classic Age brought large-scale irrigation to the Valley, and the organization of people required for this work resounded to the greater glory of Teotihuacan, making of it a place of worship to which the faithful thronged to join the black-robed priests in celebrating the mysteries that kept the world in balance — rain and fire, planting and harvesting, and the endless, mystical renewal of the holy days of the calendar.

Varying forms of the typical Maya calendar systems came into use among all the sprouting cities of Mexico — the calendar that swallowed itself, like the two-headed serpent, every 260 days and every 52 years, spinning out the revelation that everything came to an end and yet was reborn, everything changed and yet remained the same, and the circle revolved forever.

The sacrifice of human beings, dogs, birds, flowers, anything that lived, was an act in recognition and sustenance of this eternal process. The notion of sacrifice to appease angry gods is Mesopotamian, not Mesoamerican.** Angry gods are shepherds' gods, living in the lightning, and the Indians kept no flocks. The gods of Teotihuacan were in the sunlight that buttered the Valley and brought growth, and in the stars that hung like volleys of javelins in the sharp brittle air and never failed in the ceaseless repetition of their flight. The Amer-

---

*A large tribe of Amerinds living in southern Mexico and north central America, who flourished from about 60 A.D. to 800 A.D.

**Central America from the middle of Mexico to central Honduras.

37

Creation Myth of the Mayan Indians

Mayan pyramids, Chichen Itza, Yucatan. Field Museum.

This is the account of how all was in suspense, all calm, in silence, all motionless, still, and the expanse of the sky was empty.

This is the 1st account, the 1st narrative. There was neither man, nor animal, birds, fishes, crabs, trees, stones, caves, ravines, grasses, nor forests: There was only the sky.

There was nothing brought together, nothing which could make a noise, nor anything which might move, or tremble, or could make noise in the sky.

There was nothing standing; only the calm water, the placid sea, alone and tranquil. Nothing existed.

There was only immobility and silence in the darkness, in the night. Only the Creator, the Maker, Tepeu, Gucumatz, the Forefathers, were in the water surrounded with light. They were hidden under green and blue feathers, and were therefore called Gucumatz. By nature they were great sages and great thinkers. In this manner the sky existed and also the Heart of Heaven, which is the name of God and thus He is called.

Then came the word. Tepeu and Gucumatz came together in the darkness, in the night, and Tepeu and Gucumatz talked together. They talked then, discussing and deliberating; they agreed, they united their words and their thoughts.

Then while they meditated, it became clear to them that when dawn would break, man must appear. Then they planned the creation, and the growth of the trees and the thickets and the birth of life and the creation of man. Thus it was arranged in the darkness and in the night by the heart of Heaven who is called Huracan.

The 1st is called Caculha Huracan. The second is Chipi-Caculha. The 3rd is Raxa-Caculha. And these 3 are the Heart of Heaven.

Then Tepeu and Gucumatz came together; then they conferred about life and light, what they would do so that there would be light and dawn, who it would be who would provide food and sustenance.

Thus let it be done. Let the emptiness be filled! Let the water recede and make a void, let the earth appear and become solid; let it be done. Thus they spoke. Let there be light, let there be dawn in the sky and on the earth! There shall be neither glory nor grandeur in our creation and formation until the human being is made, man is formed. So they spoke.

Then the earth was created by them. So it was, in truth, that they created the earth. Earth! they said, and instantly it was made.

Like the mist, like a cloud, and like a cloud of dust was the creation, when the mountains appeared from the water; and instantly the mountains grew.

Only by a miracle, only by magic art were the mountains and valleys formed; and instantly the groves of cypresses and pines put forth shoots together on the surface of the earth.

And thus Gucumatz was filled with joy, and exclaimed: "Your coming has been fruitful, Heart of Heaven; and you, Huracan, and you, Chipa-Caculha, Raxa-Caculha!"

"Our work, our creation shall be finished," they answered.

First the earth was formed, the mountains and the valleys; the currents of water were divided, the rivulets were running freely between the hills, and the water was separated when the high mountains appeared.

Thus was the earth created, when it was formed by the Heart of Heaven, the Heart of Earth, as they are called who 1st made it fruitful, when the sky was in suspense, and the earth was submerged in the water.

So it was that they made perfect the work, when they did it after thinking and meditating upon it.

—*Popol Vuh: The Sacred Book of the Ancient Quiche Maya*. Translated from the original text by Adrian Recinos. (Norman, Okla.: University of Oklahoma Press, 1950.)

*ican gods were hungry, not angry,
hungry for the destruction of living
things that was the bassdrum beat
of the rhythm of life, the death that
brought new life. Without constant
death the life of the gods grew
weak, for was not death the ultimate objective of life, and thus its
food?*

> —*The American Heritage Book of
Indians,* pp. 42–43.

To most people of the twentieth
century, the religious beliefs and
practices of these earliest Americans
may seem crude, sometimes cruel,
superstitious, and useless. For the
earliest Americans, they were not.
Their religious beliefs and practices
were sacred to them—far more sacred
than the religious beliefs and practices
of most twentieth century Americans.
Like all religious people, their beliefs
and practices were based on their
world view—on the way they
experienced the world, the way they
viewed their relationship with whatever
God was for them, on their conception
of the origin of life and their own
origins, on the destiny of people, and
their view of the afterlife. Like all
people, they responded to the mystery
of life as they understood that mystery
and attempted to live in harmony with
the unknown, the Ultimate Mystery,
the Utterly Other, the God who made
all things possible.

*We came from beneath the
ground, the legends say, we came
from the sunrise of the east, or the
sunset of the west. We climbed up
to the light from the bowels of our
holy mountain, we climbed down
from the sky by a ladder of arrows.*

*At first there was only the god Coy-
ote or Raven, Serpent or Jaguar.
At first there was "only the calm
water, the placid sea, alone and
tranquil. Nothing existed," say the
Mayas. And at first there was only
the sea, say also the seafaring
Haida of the Northwest Coast, and
down at the volcanic tail of South
America, not surprisingly, the Ona
people have a tradition that "they
came from the north and became
isolated from their kin by a great
cataclysm, which rent their island
from the mainland."*

*In ancient times there were white
men with long black beards, say
people thousands of miles apart. A
giant black man lives in the heavens, or the woods, or the mountains, and punishes those who do
wrong. In ancient times women
ruled, because they had the magic
masks, or the magic flutes, but men
spied on them and stole their magic
away. In ancient times a beautiful
girl had a lover who came each
night but would not let her see who
he was, so she painted her hands,
or rubbed them in soot, and that
night embraced her lover again,
and the next day saw the marks of
her hands on the back of her
brother. She ran from him in horror
and he ran after her, so she turned
herself into the sun and he turned
himself into the moon, and he still
appears at night looking for her, but
she has always gone away, and the
marks of her hands are still on his
back. In the first days men despaired and lost their repose, so the
Creator gave them the tobacco and
they chewed it and gained their repose, but it only lasted a short time*

and they despaired and lost their repose again, so the Creator gave them women.

All about them the world comprehended simply by being, and so did they. Of course there was meaning in the spring stars hanging in the silver branches of the spring forest, and the autumn stars hanging in the antlers of a tall silent beast, or the terror of a storm shouting in your ear, or the dread of hunger in black winter days.

With such comprehensions, the American Indians came into existence, people of infinite differences and remarkable samenesses. Some feared the world and placated its

Sioux sun dance. Buechel Memorial Lakota Museum.

ferocity, and some worshipped with praise its goodness. Some apologized to animals they killed, and others insulted them. Some feared the dead—not so much death as the dead, with their unnatural sightless eyes and their ghosts that sprang up in the dark—and fled from the dead in panic, even while

weeping with grief, to abandon them where they died; while others hung up the dead in a place of honor in the lodging and kept them there. One insistent tone is present in all these varying examples, an awareness of the harmony of things that can be struck out of balance at any moment, even by a man's own actions. (By a knife or a stone I can bring the abnormality of death; by careful and right behavior can I keep my normal world free of such abnormalities as death and sickness?) If time is the tonic note in the story of the Indians, this theme of the world's precarious harmony is the dominant.

It underlies one of the few traits that might be applied sweepingly to most American Indians, belief in a personally acquirable magic power. The widespread concept of ownership of land in common by a related group of people might be another such trait. These attitudes were overwhelmed in emerging societies elsewhere in the world by other sets of notions drawn from other primitive world views, but they gained the ascendancy in America. Operated upon by untroubled time, they became distinctively Indian.

—*The American Heritage Book of Indians*, pp. 16–17.

The Religion of the Modern Indian

For the most part, the descendants of these earliest Americans in Canada,

A Cheyenne Creation Myth

Ceremonial Sioux catlinite pipe. Museum of the American Indian.

In the beginning there was nothing, and Maheo, the All Spirit, lived in the void. There was nothing to see, nothing to hear—only Maheo.

Because of the greatness of his Power, Maheo was not lonesome; his being was the universe. But as he moved through the endless time of nothingness, he asked himself, What good is Power, if not used?

With his Power, Maheo created a great salt lake. Out of it, he could bring all life. In the darkness of nothingness, Maheo could feel the water's coolness and taste its salty tang on his lips.

Maheo told his Power, "There should be water beings". And so he created the fish that swam, the snails that crawled in the muddy bottom, and the snow geese and ducks and coots that lived and swam on the water's surface. Maheo could hear the splashing of their feet and the flapping of their wings in the darkness.

I should like to see the things that have been created, Maheo decided. And so light began to grow and spread until it filled the sky. Maheo watched the light, and he saw the birds and the fishes, and the shellfish lying on the lake bottom. How beautiful it all is, Maheo thought in his heart.

But the birds became tired of swimming. "Then fly," said Maheo, and he waved his arms, and all the water birds flew. "How beautiful their wings are in the light," Maheo said to his Power.

Then the birds became tired of flying and requested a dry, solid place to build their nests. "So be it," answered Maheo, "but to make such a place I must have your help, for my Power will only let me make four things by myself, and I have made the water, the light, and sky air, and the peoples of the water. One of you must try to find land."

The birds all tried, but each one failed. At last the little coot tried, swimming to the bottom of the salty lake. After a long, long time he rose, with a little ball of mud on his tongue, which he dropped into Maheo's hand, for Maheo had taken the form of a man.

Maheo rolled the ball of mud between the palms of his hands, and it grew until there was almost too much for him to hold. Maheo looked for a place to set the mud, but there was nothing but water or air around him. Finally Grandmother Turtle swam over, and Maheo piled the mud on her round back. It spread out until she was hidden from sight.

"So be it," Maheo said. "Let the earth be known as our Grandmother, and let the Grandmother who carries the earth be the only being at home beneath the water, or within the earth, or above the ground."

And so it was and so it is. Grandmother Turtle and her descendents walk very slowly, for they carry the weight of the whole world on their backs.

Now there was earth as well as air and water, but the earth was barren. And Maheo said to his Power, "Our Grandmother Earth is like a woman; she should be fruitful." When Maheo said that, trees and grass sprang up, then flowers, fruits, and seeds. The birds came to rest on Grandmother Earth's hands when they were tired, and the fish came close to her sides. Maheo thought the Earth Woman very beautiful.

She should not be alone, Maheo thought. I will give her something of myself. Out of a rib from his right side, Maheo made the first man. Out of a rib from his left side, he made the first woman. In the springtime, their first child was born. Their descendents founded many tribes. Maheo is still everywhere, watching all his people. He is all good and all life; creator, guardian and teacher. We are all here because of Maheo.

—retold from the Cheyenne.

the United States, and Mexico are Christians—or participate in "the white man's religion." But they have retained a loyalty to their heritage—to the beliefs and practices of their ancestors. In the moments of tribal difficulty, in the presence of death, when there was need for tribal decisions to be made, and in their recollections of their culture, they recall and practice some of the religious ceremonies, dances, rituals, and liturgies of their revered ancestors. This is not a rejection of Christianity; it is a response to the Mystery of Life bred into the Indian psyche by centuries of living in harmony with the world as they knew and experienced it.

For Review and Discussion

1. Why are the Indians of North America called "Indians"?
2. Where did the Indians of North America come from? How did they get here? Where did the Eskimos come from? Are they also "Indians"?
3. From where did the native Hawaiians come?
4. What was the religion of the earliest Americans? Explain in detail, with examples.
5. What was the purpose of the religious rites and ceremonies of the earliest Americans? Give examples to illustrate.
6. What was the purpose of magical rites in primitive religions?
7. Why was the medicine man, or shaman, an important part of the societal structure in primitive societies?
8. Discuss the treatment of the American Indians by the invading Europeans.
9. Be sure you can define the following words:

amulet	Mesoamerica
animism	Polynesian
Aztec	shaman
Beringia Bridge	taboo
Cahokia	totem
Ice Age	tribe

For Research

1. Prepare a brief report on the discovery of Canada, the United States, and Mexico by European explorers.
2. Find out what you can about the Indian tribes that inhabited the area in which you now live.
3. Look up some data on the practice of animism in primitive societies on other continents.
4. Prepare a report on the life of the Eskimo before the twentieth century.
5. Be prepared to make an oral report on one of the following civilizations: the Olmec, the Mayan, the Aztec, the Huron, the Iroquois, or the Hopi.
6. Find out what you can about Cuzco and Machu Picchu in Peru.

3

GOSPELS
JESUS
priest
saints
mass
creed
POPE
BISHOP
NUN
DEACONS
APOSTLES
VOW
dogma

Roman Catholicism in North America

Indian culture remained virtually untouched by outside influences until Christopher Columbus, an Italian navigator sailing under the Spanish flag, landed at Guanahani in the Bahamas on October 12, 1492. After establishing a small fort in what was to become Santo Domingo, he returned to Europe in January, 1493. In autumn of the same year, he went back to his settlement with 1500 people and claimed this "New World" for Spain.

Columbus' discovery of an entirely new land mass set off a flurry of activity among the powers of Europe. Portugal, Spain, Holland, France, and England began sending expeditions to this New World to bring its treasures back to their homelands. In succeeding years, areas of influence were established: Spain controlled almost all of the southern part of North America (Florida, southern and western United States, and Mexico); France controlled Canada and the midwestern United States; and England controlled the northeastern seaboard of the United States. These territorial alignments of the great European powers shaped the economic, political, cultural, and religious history of North America.

The first religion to come to North America after Columbus' discovery was

Roman Catholicism, though at the time it was not called "Roman Catholicism." It shaped the religious and cultural life of Canada and Mexico, and eventually grew to be the largest single Church group in the United States.

Roman Catholicism Comes to North America

When Columbus stumbled on the New World, generally all of Europe was religiously aligned with the Pope in Rome. Within fifty years, a religious movement which became known as the "Reformation" divided Europe into religious enclaves. Spain and France remained "Roman" Catholic; Germany, Holland, and the Scandinavian countries largely followed Luther's lead; and the people of England became "English" Catholics when King Henry VIII rebelled against Rome.

Once the initial Reformation activity began, many other religious groups sprang up in Europe, all of them "protesting" the religious expression of Christianity as dictated by the Pope. This religious movement became known as the Protestant Reformation, and soon all religious groups not aligned with Rome became known as "Protestants" even though their expressions of Christianity varied widely among themselves. This religious movement in Europe affected the development of religion and religious expression in North America for over three hundred years.

Roman Catholic Christianity came to North America with the Spanish and

Courtesy, Chon Day

French missioners. Whenever the King of Spain authorized an expedition to the New World, he sent priests along "to contact the native peoples so that [they] might observe the manner in which may be undertaken their conversion of the Faith."* In 1523, Charles V, King of Spain, wrote to his military commander in Florida: "The chief motive you are to have and to hold in this affair is the conversion of the Indians and to this end it is proper that a religious person should accompany you."**

Spanish **conquistadors** and missionaries fanned out all over Mexico, and the southeastern, southwestern, and western boundaries of the United States as far north as the state of Washington. Wherever they

---

*From Columbus' *Journal*.

**From the Spanish records of matters concerning events in Florida at this date.

Mission San Luis Rey, San Diego, California

went, they established missions—teaching the Indians how to plant crops, build permanent homes, tan leather, run forges, tend cattle, shear sheep, dig wells, spin, weave, sew, and cook. In this process of "civilizing" the Indians, they tried to persuade them to become Christians. For the most part they were successful, even though their missions were later taken over by greedy Spanish landowners. To this day, Mexican Indians and the Spanish-speaking peoples of Mexico and the southwestern United States are predominantly Roman Catholic, however, because of the positive contributions of many heroic missionaries.

The French, as we said, settled in Canada along the St. Lawrence river. Two of their principal settlements, Montreal and Quebec, became the center for the spread of French culture. From France and the seminaries established in Montreal and Quebec, missionaries went to eastern Canada and to the Louisiana Territories as far south as New Orleans and as far east as the state of New York. Other French missioners travelled west, converting Indians to the Roman Catholic faith and establishing settlements (which were later taken over or destroyed by the invading Europeans from the east). The efforts of the French missioners were not so successful as the Spanish to the south and southwest, due in part to the differences in climate, Indian culture, and method; but the French did succeed in establishing a large Catholic population in southeastern Canada and in Louisiana, both of which are largely Catholic today.

National Shrine of the North American Martyrs, Auriesville, NY

Roman Catholicism came to the eastern seaboard of the United States from England, after the persecution of Catholics under King Henry VIII (1509-1547), Queen Elizabeth I (1558-1603), and other Protestant rulers of England. When English Roman Catholics came to "the colonies" to escape persecution, they were met with equal persecution (except in Maryland, where they established their own settlement, and in Pennsylvania, where the **Quakers** had founded a free society). Roman Catholics in the New England area and in the south were a very small minority among the Protestant groups. They numbered only about 25,000 among some four million people in the thirteen original States when the Constitution was adopted in 1788. They continued to be a small minority in the United States until the periods of great immigration from Ireland and the mainland of Europe swelled their numbers in the late nineteenth and early twentieth centuries. At the present time there are over 49,000,000 Roman Catholics in the United States, 9,000,000 in Canada, and 61,000,000 in Mexico, making Roman Catholicism the largest single denomination in North America.

What Is Roman Catholicism?

Roman Catholicism is a religious faith that expresses in words, actions, and rituals, what Roman Catholics believe about a Supreme Being, and what a person's relationship to that Supreme Being is.

Roman Catholicism is a branch of Christianity that traces its origins to the

47

time of Jesus Christ. It is called "Roman" Catholicism to distinguish it from other Christian groups who do not recognize the **bishop** of Rome, called the "**Pope,**" as head of the universal Christian Church.*

It is called "**Catholic**"** because, historically, the Christian Church called itself "catholic," not because it was everywhere (which it now is), but because it was commissioned by Jesus to preach the gospel to all people. "Go, therefore," he said, "and make disciples of all nations." (Matthew 28:19) When the religious movement called the Reformation took place, the term Roman Catholic came into vogue to designate those Christians who continued to acknowledge the Pope as the head of the universal Christian Church.

The Origin of the Christian Church

The Christian Church came into being in 33 A.D. when the special early followers of Jesus who are called **apostles**† convinced a group of

Jewish people that Jesus—who had lived among them and "went about doing good," as the Gospels say—was the **Messiah**†† promised to the Jewish people, and that God had made Jesus "Lord of the universe."

> *"Listen to these words, fellow Israelites!" [Peter said]—"Jesus of Nazareth was a man whose divine authority was clearly proven to you by all the miracles and wonders which God performed through him. You yourselves know this, for it happened here among you. In accordance with his own plan God had already decided that Jesus would be handed over to you; and you killed him by letting sinful men crucify him. . . . All the people of Israel, then, are to know for sure that this Jesus, whom you crucified, is the one that God has made Lord and Messiah!"*
> —Acts of the Apostles 2:22-24 & 36

About three thousand people accepted the message and testimony of the apostles that day and were baptized. The Christian Church was born.

The Christian Church, however, like a newborn infant, had a prehistory—a period of gestation that brought it into being. This prehistory included the history of the Jewish people and the activity of Jesus of Nazareth, a Galilean Jew, who became the best known person in the history of the Western world.

It includes the history of the Jewish people because Christianity's early

---

*The word *pope* comes from the Old English *papa* which came from Church Latin, which adapted it from the Greek word *pappas*, meaning "father." In its capitalized form it now refers almost exclusively to the Catholic bishop of Rome, who is considered the successor to Peter, the leader of Christ's apostles.

**From the Greek word *katholikos* meaning "universal."

†From the Greek word *apostolos* meaning "one who is sent."

---

††The promised and expected deliverer of the Jewish people. The word comes from the Hebrew *mashiah* meaning "anointed."

Pentecost, *by a Westphalian Master (c. 1380)*

history, theology, and religious practices were Jewish. It includes the activity of Jesus because he went around Palestine preaching an interpretation of **Judaism** different from what was being taught, and doing extraordinary things that convinced a small number of followers that he was someone special.

At first, Christianity was not a new religion; it was a movement within Judaism. But, when the followers of Jesus were unable to convince the Jewish leaders that Jesus was the promised Jewish Messiah, and were forbidden to continue saying that he was, they formed small groups of believers within the Jewish community. Eventually, they extended their activities outside of the Jewish communities, and, in a relatively short time, had formed communities of believers throughout the Middle East and in cities all along the

Mediterranean coast. As time went on, these communities developed their own theology and religious practices, and became a new religion based upon what they believed about Jesus.

Who Is Jesus for Christians?

For Christians, Jesus is the Son of God who became a human being. To understand why they believe this, a person must understand how they came to believe that a man, whom they knew and experienced as a man, was the Son of God. They came to this belief because of how they experienced him. Who was this Jesus?

Jesus was born about the year 6 B.C.* in Bethlehem, a small town about five miles south of Jerusalem. He grew up in Nazareth, in Galilee, a province in northern Palestine.

Jesus of Nazareth. *Franco Zefferelli.*

Jesus lived and worked in and around Nazareth until he was about thirty years old, when he began his preaching/teaching career. He travelled throughout Palestine talking to people about God's loving care for them; about people's need to show love and compassion for each other and especially for the poor, the sick, the blind, the lame, the sorrowful, and those alienated from society; and about the need for self-reform in thinking and acting.

In a very short time, Jesus built a reputation for wisdom and goodness (he cured the sick and the crippled, worked with the poor, and showed extraordinary understanding and

concern for those in trouble) and attracted a following that had some of the leaders of the Jewish people deeply worried.

His teaching, which was radically different from the interpretations of Jewish Law currently in vogue, aroused suspicion, then distrust, then confrontation, and finally a showdown in Jerusalem before the Jewish high court, the Sanhedrin. He was charged with blasphemy by the Sanhedrin, and turned over to the Roman rulers of Palestine. The Roman governor, Pontius Pilate, condemned Jesus to death by crucifixion.

Fifty days after Jesus' death, his close followers testified that Jesus was no longer dead—he was, they said, alive and living among them in his "risen" body. They said that three

---

*The dating of Jesus' birth "about 6 B.C. **[before Christ]**" comes from recent historical research.

The Risen Christ, *Abbey of St. Maurice, Valais, Switzerland.*

days after his death he rose from the dead, came among them from time to time, talked with them, and shared meals with them. They said that he had commissioned them "to make disciples of all the nations," and that they should "baptize them in the name of the Father, and of the Son, and of the Holy Spirit. Teach them," Jesus said, "to carry out everything I have commanded you. And know that I am with you always until the end of the world" [The Gospel according to Matthew 28:19-20]. This teaching is contained in the **Gospels**—four different but complementary accounts of the teaching and activity of Jesus.

What the Gospels really say is that the Jesus the people knew was really the Son of God who became a human being to save the world from sin. This is the heart and soul of Christian belief. It is what makes Christianity different from all other religions.

Before the world was created, the Word already existed; he was with God, and he was the same as God. From the very beginning, the Word was with God. Through him God made all things; not one thing in all creation was made without him. The Word had life in himself, and this life brought light to men. The light shines in the darkness, and the darkness has never put it out.

God sent his messenger, a man named John, who came to tell people about the light. He came to tell them, so that all should hear the message and believe. He himself was not the light; he came to tell about the light. This was the real light, the light that comes into the world and shines on all men.

The Word, then, was in the world. God made the world through him, yet the world did not know him. He came to his own country, but his own people did not receive him. Some, however, did receive him and believed in him; so he gave them the right to become God's children. They did not become God's children by natural means, by being born as the children of a human father; God himself was their Father.

The Word became a human being and lived among us. We saw his glory, full of grace and truth. This was the glory which he received as the Father's only Son.

John told about him. He cried out, "This is the one I was talking about when I said, 'He comes after me, but he is greater than I am, because he existed before I was born.' "

Out of the fullness of his grace he has blessed us all, giving us one blessing after another. God gave the Law through Moses; but grace and truth came through Jesus Christ. No one has ever seen God. The only One, who is the same as God and is at the Father's side, he has made him known.

—The Gospel according to John 1:1-18

The Growth of the Christian Church

The first community of Christians began in Jerusalem. Shortly, through the efforts of the twelve apostles and others, Christian communities spread throughout Palestine, Syria, Egypt, Greece, modern Turkey, North Africa, Italy, and Spain.

Within three hundred years, Christianity was the dominant religion in the Roman Empire in the lands that bordered on the Mediterranean Sea. In the next six hundred years, it spread throughout modern Europe. In the Arab countries and all along the North African coast it was supplanted by Islam, the religion founded by Mohammed (570–632 A.D.), and in the rest of the Empire it divided into two major groups: the Eastern Church, later called the Orthodox Church, centered in Constantinople (modern Istanbul in northwest Turkey), and the Western Church, centered in Rome.

From about 1000 A.D. to 1500 A.D., the Christian Church grew and flourished in the West, until Martin Luther (1483–1546 A.D.), an Augustinian monk from Germany, questioning some of the practices of the Western Church under the leadership of the Popes in Rome, led some people into an interpretation of Christianity which differed from the interpretation of "Roman" Christians. His separation from Rome was the first of many breaks from Roman authority, the chief of which (in addition to Luther's), were the English separation led by King Henry VIII, and the Swiss separation led by John Calvin (1509–1564 A.D.), a French theologian.

These major separations (or reforms, as they were called), led to many reforms or separations, most of which were reforms of the reforms.

In a short time, Christianity in Europe was divided into Roman Catholic and Protestant groups, and

Gallarus Oratory (beehive hut), Ireland (c. 500 AD)

Chapel Santa Maria Assunta, Poschiavo, Switzerland

the Protestant groups were divided into four principal interpretations:

*1. The **Lutheran** groups followed Martin Luther's rejection of those parts of Roman Catholicism which he felt contradicted the Bible.*

*2. The **Reformed** Protestants retained in their religions only those things in Roman Catholicism which they believed were expressly contained in the Bible. Such groups as the Calvinists, Presbyterians, and Puritans, reflecting austere simplicity in their religious services, are outstanding examples of these groups.*

*3. The **Radical** Protestants departed even further from Roman Catholicism and rejected those aspects of Lutheranism and Calvinism which had any resemblance to Rome. They rejected all formulas, insisted on "a new birth in the Spirit" as shown by strict adherence to rigid moral laws and the rejection of infant baptism as valid. They tended to take Scripture very literally and tried to form ideal communities with common ownership of all goods. The Baptists, Anabaptists, Mennonites, Unitarians, Quakers, and Congregationalists are typical of the Radical Protestant groups.*

*4. The **English** Protestants retained almost all of the externals of Roman Catholicism except papal authority and the Latin language until King Edward VI (1547–1553) and Elizabeth (1558–1603) moved the English Church more and more toward Continental Protestantism. The Anglicans and the Methodists*

Basle Minister, Switzerland

St. Donat Church, Zadar, Yugoslavia (c. 1450)

represent the two forms of English Protestantism; one nearly "Roman" in its worship, the other clearly anti-Roman in its practice.

As Protestant groups moved further and further from the Roman position, they expressed an entire spectrum of belief and practice ranging from nearly exact copies of Romanism to total rejection of Roman traditions. Many Protestant groups were formed in protest to existing Protestant practices, but all of them retained two basic elements of protest against Rome: opposition to the papacy and to the Roman interpretation of the faith. These two remain characteristic of all Protestant groups.

Not all of these Protestant groups, of course, arose in the sixteenth century. The successful development of these divergent expressions of the meaning of Christ took many years and drew more and more people away from the expression of Christianity that was peculiar to the Roman Church, which had been "The Faith" for twelve hundred years. Where once Western Civilization had been unified in its religious expression—however inadequate it had been from time to time—now this civilization was fragmented into dozens of expressions of faith, each reflecting the special theological and cultural peculiarities of its adherents.

—Ronald J. Wilkins, *The Emerging Church*, (Dubuque, Iowa: Wm. C. Brown Company Publishers, 1968), pp. 182–183.

From the time of Martin Luther to the present, Christianity has been expressed in three principal ways: Roman Catholicism, Eastern Orthodoxy, and Protestantism. These three forms of Christianity are found in Canada, the United States, and Mexico.*

The Principal Beliefs of Roman Catholicism

As we said above, the principal belief of Christianity is that Jesus Christ is the Son of God who became a human being to save people from sin. From this, there follow other beliefs

---

*There are over four hundred different expressions of Protestantism in North America.

which are basic to Christianity as a whole, and some which are peculiar to specific expressions of Christianity. Of these, some are based on a particular denomination's interpretation of the Christian scriptures, some are based on traditions coming from early Christianity, and some are based on the cultural and philosophical outlook of theologians working out of a particular religious expession of Christianity.

The simplest way to summarize the beliefs of Roman Catholicism is to quote the "**Nicene Creed**,"* an expression of the substance of the Christian faith as it is expressed in Roman Catholicism:

---

*This formula of faith was drawn up at the Council of Nicaea in 325 A.D. Many Protestant denominations also use this creed for their expression of what they believe. They differ from Roman Catholics in understanding what some of the expressions in the creed mean.

We believe in One God, the Father, the Almighty, maker of heaven and earth, of all that is seen and unseen.

We believe in one Lord, Jesus Christ, the only Son of God, eternally begotten of the Father, God from God, Light from Light, true God from true God, begotten, not made, one in Being with the Father. Through him all things were made.

For us men and for our salvation he came down from heaven; by the power of the Holy Spirit he was born of the Virgin Mary, and became man. For our sake he was crucified under Pontius Pilate; he suffered, died, and was buried. On the third day he rose again in fulfillment of the Scriptures; he ascended into heaven and is seated at the right hand of the Father. He will come again in glory to judge the living and

13th century St. Luzius Shrine, Cathedral of Chur, Grisons, Switzerland.

*the dead, and his kingdom will
have no end.*

*We believe in the Holy Spirit, the
Lord, the giver of life, who pro-
ceeds from the Father and the
Son. With the Father and the Son
he is worshipped and glorified.
He has spoken through the
prophets.*

*We believe in one, holy, catholic,
and apostolic Church. We acknowledge one baptism for the
forgiveness of sins. We look for
the resurrection of the dead, and
the life of the world to come.*

A **creed** is an expression of faith.
From that expression come
explanations of what a person, or a
religious community believes. It is in
these explanations that Christian
denominations differ. Roman Catholics
explain what they believe in their
"**dogmas**" which are official
statements about the meaning of
particular aspects of their Christian
faith.

Among the principal dogmas of
Roman Catholicism are:

1. The Trinity. All religions accept
the reality of God as a given fact.
Roman Catholics (and almost all other
Christians) believe that God is
"**Trinity**"; that is, that God exists in
three Persons which are one Divine
Nature (or essence), and therefore are
equally eternal and almighty. They
believe that the three Persons are
distinct from each other, yet each
Person is the One God.

Admittedly, this dogma is hard to
explain—and even harder to
understand. No Christian says he
understands it, or can explain it fully. It
is the Christian mystery, *par*

excellence, and the primary and
distinctive aspect of the Christian
concept of God.

It is called a "mystery," however,
not because it is difficult to explain and
understand, but because it is, so
Christians believe, a revelation to
people by God of Himself. This is what
is meant by a "mystery" in Christian
belief.

Generally, Christians believe that
God is Trinity because they believe
that Jesus is the Son of God who
revealed that God is Father, distinct
from himself, and that God, as Father,
would send "another" Paraclete (an
advocate or helper) distinct from
himself "who will instruct you in
everything."

*Thomas said to him, "Lord, we
do not know where you are going;
so how can we know the way to get
there?"*

*Jesus answered him, "I am the
way, the truth, and the life; no one
goes to the Father except by me.
Now that you have known me," he
said to them, "you will know my
Father also, and from now on you
do know him and you have seen
him. . . . Whoever has seen me
has seen the Father. Why, then, do
you say, 'Show us the Father'? Do
you not believe, Philip, that I am in
the Father and the Father is in me?
. . . I will ask the Father, and he
will give you another Helper, who
will stay with you forever. He is the
Spirit, who reveals the truth about
God. The world cannot receive him,
because it cannot see him or know
him. But you know him, because he
remains with you and is in you."*

—The Gospel according to John,
14:5-7, 9-10, 16-17

2. Revelation. Because of what they believe about Jesus, Christians believe that God revealed himself in Person. Christians believe that God reveals himself also in what they call their "**scriptures**" (or **Bible**, as it is commonly called) which, for them, is God's written word.

The Christian Scriptures are divided into two main parts: the Old Testament and the New Testament. The Old Testament consists of forty-six books in the Roman Catholic Bible and is substantially the same as the Hebrew Bible. It contains God's revelation of himself in the history of the Jewish people. The New Testament is, for Christians, God's revelation of himself in Christ. It contains twenty-seven books, or parts: four Gospels, twenty-one **epistles**, or letters, one history book, called the **Acts of the Apostles**, and one prophetic book, called "Revelation."

The Gospels, as we have said, are four different, but complementary, accounts of the words and actions of Jesus. The epistles are letters written by some of the apostles and other early Church leaders to the first Christian communities, advising them how to live the Christian life. The Acts of the Apostles is a sketchy account of the spread of Christianity in the early years. It deals chiefly with the activities of St. Peter and St. Paul. Revelation is a book about the triumph of Christ in Christians in the face of persecutions suffered toward the end of the first century. These materials were brought together into a single collection sometime between the end of the first century after Christ and the middle of the second.

The materials in the New Testament were selected by the early Church

St. Matthew the Evangelist. *Wettingen Abbey, Baden, Switzerland.*

leaders and added to the Hebrew scriptures to form "the book of Christians."* They were selected because they most accurately portrayed who Jesus is and what he means for people. They are believed to be inspired by God,** and, as such, are what God wants people to know about himself as revealed by Christ. For Christians, their scriptures are not simply revered writings; they are sacred and inspired. They are, for Christians, in a class by themselves.

Roman Catholics believe that their scriptures are part of the Church's tradition and constitute the norm upon which Christian belief and Christian living are based. They believe that the Church exists apart from the scriptures (the Church existed before the New Testament was compiled, just as the Jewish religion existed before the Old Testament was brought together) and is the guardian and the interpreter of the scriptures for the people.

Hence there exist a close connection and communication between sacred tradition and sacred Scripture. For both of them, flowing from the same divine wellspring, in certain way merge into a unity and tend toward the same end. For sacred Scripture is the word of God inasmuch as it is consigned to writing under the inspiration of the divine Spirit. To the successors of the apostles, sacred tradition hands on in its full purity God's word, which was entrusted to the apostles by Christ the Lord and the Holy Spirit. Thus, led by the light of the Spirit of truth, these successors can in their preaching preserve this word of God faithfully, explain it, and make it more widely known. Consequently, it is not from sacred Scripture alone that the Church draws her certainty about everything which has been revealed.

*The first Christians were all Jews—for them, the Hebrew Scriptures were already a part of God's revelation. The addition of their own sacred writings indicated that they believed the Old Testament promises were fulfilled in Christ.

**Christians believe that somehow God guided the writers of the various materials in both the Old and the New Testaments in what they wrote without interfering with their natural abilities. They also believe that God guided the Church leaders in their selection of materials that were to be included in the scriptures.

Therefore both sacred tradition and sacred scripture are to be accepted and venerated with the same sense of devotion and reverence. . . .

Those divinely revealed realities which are contained and presented in sacred Scripture have been committed to writing under the inspiration of the Holy Spirit. Holy Mother Church, relying on the belief of the apostles, holds that the books of both the Old and New Testament in their entirety, with all their parts, are sacred and canonical because, having been written under the inspiration of the Holy Spirit they have God as their author and have been handed on as such to the Church herself.
—The Documents of Vatican II, "Dogmatic Constitution on Divine Revelation" nos. 7, 9, 11.

3. Life after Death. Roman Catholics, like all other Christians, believe that there is life after earthly death. They believe this because they believe that Jesus rose from the dead.

Now, since our message is that Christ has been raised from death, how can some of you say that the dead will not be raised to life? If that is true, it means that Christ was not raised; and if Christ has not been raised from death, then we have nothing to preach and you have nothing to believe. More than that, we are shown to be lying about God, because we said that he raised Christ from death—but if it is true that the dead are not raised to life, then he did not raise Christ. For if the dead are not raised, neither has Christ been raised. And if Christ has not been raised, then your faith is a delusion and you are still lost in your sins. It would also mean that the believers in Christ who have died are lost. If our hope in Christ is good for this life only and no more, then we deserve more pity than anyone else in all the world.
—The First Epistle of Paul to the Corinthians, 15:12-19

Christians do not know what their life after earthly death will be like—they can only describe it in earthly images. What they do believe is that people will live forever (that is why they call it "eternal life"), sharing God's life as human beings with human bodies and the life force they call "souls," in a risen dimension of existence without the limitations of their present earthly existence:

Then I saw a new heaven and a new earth. The first heaven and the first earth disappeared, and the sea vanished. And I saw the Holy City, the new Jerusalem, coming down out of heaven from God, prepared and ready, like a bride dressed to meet her husband. I heard a loud voice speaking from the throne: "Now God's home is with mankind! He will live with them, and they shall be his people. God himself will be with them, and he will be their God. He will wipe away all tears from their eyes. There will be no more death, no more grief or crying or pain. The old things have disappeared."
—The Book of Revelation, 21:1-4

4. Salvation. Roman Catholics believe that because Jesus, as the Son of God, became a human being, he rescued creation from a non-divine existence. Because he did so, Roman Catholics believe that all people are saved in Christ, and that all people are called to share God's Divine Life on earth and in eternity in their risen dimension of existence.

Roman Catholics also believe, as we said above, that Christ also saves people from moral evil and the consequences of moral evil (or **sin**, as Christians call it) if they follow his teaching about how life should be lived:

His divine power has given us everything we need to live a godly life through our knowledge of the one who called us to share his own glory and goodness. In this way he has given us precious and very great promises, in order that by receiving what he has promised you may escape from the destructive passion that exists in the world, and come to share the divine nature. For this very reason, do your best to add goodness to your faith; and to your goodness add knowledge; to your knowledge add self-control; to your self-control add endurance; to your endurance add godliness; to your godliness add brotherly love; and to your brotherly love add love. These are the qualities you need, and if you have them in abundance they will make you active and effective in your knowledge of our Lord Jesus Christ. But whoever does not have them is so short-sighted that he cannot see, and has forgotten that his past sins have been washed away.

So then, my brothers, try even harder to make God's call and his choice of you a permanent experience; for if you do so you will never fall away. In this way you will be
given the full right to enter the eternal Kingdom of our Lord and Savior Jesus Christ.

—The Second Epistle of Peter 1:3-11

5. Papal Authority. Roman Catholics believe that the bishop of Rome (the Pope) is the supreme head of the universal Christian Church. (As a practical matter, of course, the Pope is acknowledged as supreme head of the universal Church only by Roman Catholics, and is, in fact, the supreme head only of the Roman Catholic Church.) They believe that he, as

St. Peter. *Cathedral of Coire, Switzerland.*

62

Pope, has a **primacy of jurisdiction** and the power to teach religious truth without error. According to Roman Catholic belief, the Pope always acts as head of the Church—and not simply as another bishop or as the "first bishop"—and that he is preserved from error in matters of faith by special divine grace.

Roman Catholics believe this because they believe that Jesus Christ founded the Church as a visible society under the authority of the apostles, and appointed Simon Peter as the head of the apostles, according to the Christian scriptures:

Pope John Paul II

"And so I tell you, Peter: [said Jesus] you are a rock, and on this rock foundation I will build my Church, and not even death will ever be able to overcome it. I will give you the keys of the Kingdom of heaven; what you prohibit on earth will be prohibited in heaven, and what you permit on earth will be permitted in heaven."

—The Gospel according to Matthew 16:18-19

"Simon, Simon! Listen! Satan has received permission to test all of you, to separate the good from the bad, as a farmer separates the wheat from the chaff. But I have prayed for you, Simon [said Jesus], that your faith will not fail. And when you turn back to me, you must strengthen your brothers."

—The Gospel according to Luke 22:31-32

Because Peter was bishop of Rome when he died and because no one else ever claimed the same authority as Peter as head of the Church, Roman Catholics believe that the Pope, as bishop of Rome, succeeds Peter in his unique role as supreme head of the universal Christian Church.

There are many other things that Roman Catholics believe, of course, which follow from their acceptance of Jesus as the Son of God. The above illustrate the Roman Catholic understanding of who and what God is, what his relationship to people is, and what people's relationship to God is. How this relationship is expressed in Roman Catholicism can best be understood by looking at some of the religious practices of Roman Catholics.

Religious Practices of Roman Catholics

Religious practices are actions by which a person or a community of persons expresses its relationship to whatever God is for the person or the community. Because Christians are supposed to relate to God as a loving Father who sent his Son to bring people to him, Christian religious practices generally attempt to reflect this relationship.

In Roman Catholicism, the principal religious act is The **Liturgy** of the **Eucharist**, commonly called "The Mass.''* It is, according to Roman Catholics, the essential activity of the Roman Catholic Church which gives the clearest expression of the nature of the Roman Catholic Church: the worshipping community of Christ, the eternal highpriest.

Rightly, then, the liturgy is considered as an exercise of the priestly office of Jesus Christ. In the liturgy the sanctification of man is manifested by signs perceptible to the senses, and is effected in a way

---

Liturgy means official, public ceremonies of worship. *Eucharist,* from the Greek word for thanksgiving, refers directly to the celebration of the Lord's Supper—the celebration of the last **Passover** meal, or **Seder,** by Jesus with his disciples before the Crucifixion.

which is proper to each of these signs; in the liturgy full public worship is performed by the Mystical Body of Jesus Christ, that is, by the Head and His members.

From this it follows that every liturgical celebration, because it is an action of Christ the priest and of His Body the Church, is a sacred action surpassing all others. No other action of the Church can match its claim to efficacy, nor equal the degree of it.

— *The Documents of Vatican II*, "The Constitution on the Sacred Liturgy," no. 7.

The Mass has two distinct parts united in one sacred ceremony: The Liturgy of the Word and The Liturgy of the Eucharist. The Liturgy of the Word consists in prayers, responses, songs, readings from the Bible centering around a particular theme, and a homily, or instruction, by the minister of worship. The first readings are from either the Old Testament, or from the epistles, the Acts of the Apostles, or Revelation; the second reading is always from one of the Gospels.

The Liturgy of the Eucharist, which contains the principal action of the Mass, recalls the **Lord's Supper** and, in a solemn prayer-action, follows the direction of Jesus who

having taken bread, he blessed, broke, and gave it to his disciples, and said, "This is my body which is given for many; do this in remembrance of me." In like manner also the cup after the meal, saying, "This cup is the new **covenant** in my blood."

—Luke 22:19-20

The Liturgy of the Eucharist concludes with the reception of the consecrated bread (and sometimes the wine) which Roman Catholics call "The Communion."

The significant thing about this aspect of Roman Catholic belief and practice is that Roman Catholics believe that the consecrated bread (and wine) really is the body and blood of Christ. For them, it is not a symbol, a recollection of Jesus' actions only, or a sign of fraternal union among the members. It is, as Roman Catholics say, "the body, blood, soul, and divinity of our Lord, Jesus Christ." Because of this belief, Roman Catholics believe that the Mass is the sacrificial meal of the new covenant they believe Jesus established with God.

The Sacraments

The second most important religious practice in the Roman Catholic Church is what Roman Catholics call "the **sacraments**." The sacraments are, for Roman Catholics, "the visible signs of Christ acting in his Church in the lives of his people in the same way he acted in the lives of the people with whom he associated himself while on earth."*

The sacraments are actions (things done and words said) of the Church, as Church, which signify Christ acting in the lives of individuals in the critical, or special, moments of their lives. In the Roman Catholic Church, there are seven sacraments:

*According to St. Paul, the Christian Church is the body of Christ. "All of you are Christ's body, and each one is a part of it." (The First Letter of Paul to the Corinthians 12:27.)

Baptism. Baptism is the initiating ceremony of immersion in, or pouring on of, water whereby a person is incorporated into the Christian community.

Confirmation. Confirmation is the sign of the seal of the Holy Spirit, in which a person is "signed," or marked, with blessed oil on the forehead signifying his adult status in the Catholic Community.

The Eucharist. This sacrament is the presence of Christ under the appearances of bread and wine as the substantial nourishment of the Catholic Christian. It is ordinarily received during Mass, but may be received any time under certain circumstances.

Bishop ordaining permanent deacon

The Sacrament of Reconciliation. This sacrament, known commonly as "Confession," is a sign of the forgiveness of sin. Because it is a public act of worship, a person confesses his sins to the priest as minister of the Church who pronounces the words of forgiveness in the name of the Church.

The Sacrament of the Sick. This sacrament is a sign of Christ's concern for and healing of those seriously sick and those in danger of death from accident or age.

The Sacrament of Matrimony. The wedding ceremony, witnessed by a priest or other authorized minister, is a sign of Christ's action in the married life of the couple marrying, and a sign of love and a sign of life for the partners in marriage.

The Sacrament of Orders. In this sacrament a person is ordained to fulfill the special sacramental ministry of the Roman Catholic Church as its official representative in liturgical functions. Every ordained minister in the Roman Catholic Church is called a priest. Those who are specially consecrated as "chief priest" in a diocese, or area, of the Roman Catholic Church with jurisdictional powers are called "bishops."

Other Religious Acts

There are other religious acts in the Roman Catholic Church such as special Masses of burial, special blessings, the official prayers of the priests called "the Divine Office," and semi-liturgical actions which are devotional, for example, the celebration of special feast days in particular areas of the world or special devotions honoring one or another special Roman Catholic aspect of the religious life.

In addition, there are private devotions of one kind or another, private celebrations of the feasts of saints, the prayer life of individual Roman Catholics, pilgrimages, shrines, the building of Churches, and the sending of missionaries to other countries.

Perhaps the most visible sign of Roman Catholic devotional life is the devotion to Mary, the Mother of Jesus. Although it is often misunderstood and misinterpreted as "worship" of Mary, it is not. It is, rather, a sign of respect for

Madonna with Child. *Ohrid (c. 1425). National Museum, Belgrade, Yugoslavia*

and special dedication to Mary as the mother of Jesus. Like the respect paid to any person living or dead, the respect paid is in proportion to the worth of the person and the contribution of that person to the good of the world. In Roman Catholic eyes, no one has had such personal worth (outside of Jesus, of course) nor contributed so much to the good of the World as Mary as "Mother of God."

Roman Catholic devotion to Mary, like the celebration of the feast days of Roman Catholic "**saints**," is based on the doctrine of "the communion of saints." This doctrine, which stems directly from the Roman Catholic belief in life after death, maintains that there is a fellowship in faith and concern which extends beyond the grave, to those who have already attained the purpose of their having been created: union with God.

Religious Men and Women and Catholic Schools

Two other things closely associated with Roman Catholic life in North America are religious **sisters** and Catholic schools.

Catholic sisters are one part of a larger group called "**religious**" in Roman Catholicism. Religious are people—male and female, priests and non-priests—who dedicate their lives to special religious work in a community, or congregation, organized to accomplish a particular social goal, such as teaching, nursing, mission

work, or social service. They make **vows**, or solemn promises, of poverty, chastity, and obedience. That is, they renounce ownership of private property (things are owned in common by the community or congregation), give up the right to marry, and promise to obey the rules of the group to which they belong as long as they are members of the group. There are about 220,000 religious in North America: 40,000 religious men and 180,000 religious women, called nuns, or "sisters."

There are about 9,000 Catholic elementary schools in North America with about 3 million students. There are about 1700 Catholic high schools with about 800,000 students.* There are about 260 Catholic colleges and universities with about 400,000 students.** Their purpose is to project a Christian philosophy of life into learning. Catholics believe that religion, at the very least, is as important as any other culture-shaping aspect of learning; hence, it should not be ignored. They also believe that parents should have an alternative choice in selecting schools for their children and that Catholic schools give them that choice.

Catholic schools were begun in North America in 1640 by the Jesuits in Maryland. (This does not include, of course, the schools begun by all the early missioners to teach Indians the skills needed to begin a new life-style.)

---

*These figures do not include the private Catholic schools in Mexico which enroll about 400,000 students in various grade levels.

**Other religious groups such as the Lutherans, Baptists, Episcopalians, and Mormans also have "religious" schools.

St. Elizabeth Ann Seton (1774–1821)

Parochial, or parish schools, were begun by Elizabeth Seton, a recently canonized saint in the Roman Catholic Church, in 1810. They were made a part of the Catholic system in the United States in 1843 when the Catholic bishops directed the pastors (priests in charge of parishes) to establish a parish school wherever possible. Schools staffed by priests and religious were, of course, an integral part of the Catholic communities in Canada and Mexico from the very beginning. Catholic schools were banned in Mexico in the 1920's, but there are many "private" schools in Mexico today staffed by priests, religious, and lay people which carry on the traditions of Catholic education.

Roman Catholic Moral Life

Roman Catholic moral life, like the moral life of any Christian group, is based on the teachings of the New Testament. The New Testament, however, according to Christian belief, does not present a complete ethical system; it presents, rather, a philosophy, or attitude, about living which serves as the base for moral decisions. This base, according to

Christian belief, was established by Jesus when he responded to a question about living a moral life by saying:

"What do the Scriptures say? How do you interpret them?" [The man] replied
"Love the Lord your God with all your heart, with all your soul, with all your strength, and with all your mind"; and "Love your neighbor as you love yourself."
"You are right, "Jesus replied; do this and you will live."

—The Gospel according to Luke 10:26-28

In other words, according to Jesus, the moral base for Christian decision-making is love of God and love of

neighbor. It is so much so that St. Paul, the first and greatest Christian theologian, did not hesitate to say:

Whoever loves his fellow man has obeyed the Law. The commandments, "Do not commit adultery; do not murder; do not steal; do not covet"—all these, and any others besides, are summed up in the one command, "Love your neighbor as yourself." Whoever loves his neighbor will never do him wrong. To love, then, is to obey the whole Law.

—The Epistle of Paul to the Romans 13:8-10

I may be able to speak the languages of men and even of angels, but if I have not love, my speech is no more than a noisy gong or a clanging bell. I may have the gift of inspired preaching; I may have all knowledge and understand all secrets; I may have all the faith needed to move mountains—but if I have not love, I am nothing. I may give away everything I have, and even give up my body to be burned—but if I have not love, it does me no good.

Love is patient and kind; love is not jealous, or conceited, or proud; love is not ill-mannered, or selfish, or irritable; love does not keep a record of wrongs; love is not happy with evil, but is happy with the truth. Love never gives up: its faith, hope, and patience never fail.

Love is eternal. There are inspired messages, but they are temporary; there are gifts of speaking, but they will cease; there is knowledge, but it will pass. For our gifts of knowledge and of inspired messages are only partial; but when what is perfect comes, then what is partial will disappear.

When I was a child, my speech, feelings, and thinking were all those of a child; now that I am a man, I have no more use for childish ways. What we see now is like the dim image in a mirror; then we shall see face to face. What I know now is only partial; then it will be complete, as complete as God's knowledge of me.

Meanwhile these three remain: faith, hope, and love; and the greatest of these is love.

—The First Epistle of Paul to the Corinthians 13:11-13

Roman Catholic morality attempts to reflect this basic moral principle. It is based on respect for God, for oneself, for one's neighbor, and for life, for the dignity of people, for the environment, and for justice.

But, because the Gospels present a philosophy for living and an attitude toward life, rather than hard and fast answers for *every* moral contingency facing Christians in the special circumstances of their lives, Roman Catholics believe that Jesus appointed his apostles and their successors as his representatives, and gave them the responsibility of preaching the gospel and helping people make it live in their lives.

That is why, for Roman Catholics, their bishops "speak with authority in matters of faith and morals," and why Roman Catholics listen attentively to the bishops and follow their lead when they speak, or teach, about moral concerns in light of the basic teachings of the New Testament:

> *Thanks to this belief, the Church can anchor the dignity of human nature against all tides of opinion, for example, those which undervalue the human body or idolize it. By no human law can the personal dignity and liberty of man be so aptly safeguarded as by the gospel of Christ which has been entrusted to the Church.*
> —*The Documents of Vatican II,* "Pastoral Constitution on the Church in the Modern World," no. 41.

But Roman Catholics are not supposed to follow the teachings of their bishops blindly. They have intelligence, free will, and a conscience with which they are to make judgments

about the rightness or wrongness of any action, and to follow that judgment in making a decision to act or not to act. But intelligence and conscience must be informed; that is, there must be knowledge of what is right and the will to do what is right. If they are not, an intelligent choice is not made, or a selfish choice is made based on wrong or inadequate information.

Because Roman Catholics believe that Christ promised to be with them and to protect his Church from evil, they believe that the first source of knowledge concerning faith and morals based on the teachings of Christ is the teaching of the Church as presented by their bishops. The second source of knowledge about what is right and what is wrong in human conduct are the recognized theologians of the Roman Catholic Church and competent theologians of other Christian denominations; Catholic publications which reflect the teaching of the bishops; religious education; the instructions given by their priests; and the public and private discussions held by informed people on the moral problems facing Roman Catholics in a pluralistic society. Informed Roman Catholics make use of all these sources in making decisions on the morality of their actions.

The Structure of the Roman Catholic Church

For Roman Catholics, the Church is the People of God united in fellowship with Christ in honoring God. Because the Roman Catholic Church is also a

social reality, it has developed an organizational structure which enables it to carry out its purpose.

The organization of the Roman Catholic Church is based upon the division of functional ministries and territorial areas. Ministerially, the Roman Catholic Church is divided into laity (non-ordained believers, who give aid to and serve one another) and clergy (the ordained, who administer the sacraments). The clergy is divided into **deacons**, priests, and bishops.* Deacons are those who are ordained to perform certain liturgical or ministerial functions not reserved for priests. Priests are ordained in the Roman Catholic Church to preach the gospel, preside at the Eucharistic Liturgy, and minister to the special spiritual needs of the faithful as ministers of certain sacraments and leaders of certain liturgical functions. Bishops are the "principal priests" in the Roman Catholic Church with ministerial powers of the full priesthood because they share directly in the ministry of the apostles by direct succession (priests are their designated helpers), and with jurisdictional powers over a particular area of the Church. The Pope as chief bishop has jurisdictional authority over the entire Church.**

---

*This division does not signify a difference in degree—a bishop, for example, is not "more Catholic" than a priest. It signifies a difference in service since all Christians share in the priesthood of Christ through baptism.

Certain bishops in the Roman Catholic Church are designated "cardinals**." These are bishops who act as special counselors to the Pope in administering the affairs of the Church.

Eastern Rite Roman Catholics

The worldwide Roman Catholic Church is divided into dioceses, or areas, governed by a bishop. A diocese is divided into parishes, or local worshipping communities, each of which has an ordained priest as designated pastor who is in charge of the parish. There are about 1500 Roman Catholic dioceses in the world with about 165 in the United States, 69 in Canada and 68 in Mexico

In addition to these territorial diocesan divisions, the Roman Catholic Church is divided into the Western Rite Churches and the Eastern Rite Churches. The Eastern Rite Churches are those Roman Catholic communities who follow what is called "the Eastern rites" in their liturgies, customs, and laws. There are about 10 million Eastern Rite Catholics in the world, of whom about 400,000 live in North America, mostly in the eastern half of the United States.

As we have said, a rite, as used in relation to religious practices, is a formal or ceremonial act, or way of doing something prescribed or customary. When the term *Eastern Rite Catholic* is used, it refers to those Catholics who celebrate their liturgies in ceremonies derived from the customs and practices of the early Church in the eastern part of the Roman Empire—roughly those areas east of modern Yugoslavia. The principal Eastern rites are the Alexandrian, Antiochean, Byzantine, Chaldean, and Armenian. Each of these has subdivisions reflecting particular aspects of the culture of the country in which they are found, for example, the Maronite rite is basically Antiochean, and the Melkite rite is basically Byzantine.

Eastern Rite Catholics have a common bond of faith, sacraments, doctrine, and allegiance to the Pope with Western Rite Catholics, sometimes called Roman, or Latin, Rite Catholics. They have the same Eucharistic liturgy, but celebrate it, as we said above, in a manner and with customs that stem from the ancient liturgies of the

Lighting traditional Easter candles

75

Eastern Church. They have "Eastern Rite" bishops, their own dioceses, their own Eastern rite priests, and some customs different from Western Rite Catholics, such as married priests, certain special feast days and special devotions, and special religious symbols that are more meaningful for them than Western Rite symbols.

Eastern Rite Catholics came to North America around the year 1900, mainly because of religious persecution. At the present time, the principal Eastern Rite Catholic communities in North America are the Ruthenian (Ukrainian) Catholics with over 300,000, the Maronite (Lebanese) with over 40,000, the Italo-Greek (from northern Italy and Sicily) with over 20,000, the Melkite (Egyptian) with about 25,000, the Romanian with over 7,000, the Armenian with about 4,000, the Syrian with roughly 4,000, worshipping principally in Maronite and Melkite Churches, and small groups of other Eastern Rite Catholics, such as the Russian and the Chaldean.

Conclusion

The 122 million Roman Catholics in Canada, the United States, and Mexico are joined with over 500 million other Roman Catholics throughout the world in faith, worship, morality, and general religious practices. They include people of every age, race, culture, ability, social position, education, financial standing, and political persuasion. They form one part of the worldwide Christian Church which accepts Jesus as God's Son, the Second Person of the Trinity, who came, Christians believe, to lead people to God.

For Review and Discussion

1. How did Roman Catholicism come to North America?
2. What is Roman Catholicism? How did this branch of Christianity happen to be called "Roman" and "Catholic"?
3. Name, and explain in your own words, the principal beliefs and practices of Roman Catholics.
4. Why do Roman Catholics believe that the Pope is the head of the universal Church?
5. With what other religious practices of Roman Catholics not mentioned in your books are you familiar?
6. Why do Roman Catholics have "their own" schools?
7. What is the basis for Roman Catholic moral life? Explain. Why do Roman Catholic bishops play such an important role in the moral decisions of Catholics?
8. What are "Eastern Rite" Catholics? Explain.
9. Be sure that you can define the following words:

A.D.

apostle	deacon	monk	sacrament
bishop	epistle	nun	salvation
cardinal	Eucharist	Orthodox	scripture
Catholic	Gospel	Pope	sin
Communion	liturgy	priest	sister
conquistador	Mass	Protestant	Trinity
creed	Messiah	rite	vows

For Research

1. Prepare a report on the discovery of America. Include theories about Pre-Columbian activity. Use maps to pinpoint locations.
2. Prepare a brief report on either the Spanish activity in Mexico and the southern United States, the French activity in Canada and the central United States, or the English and Dutch activity in the northeastern United States. Include the sixteenth, seventeenth, and eighteenth centuries.
3. Read The Acts of the Apostles, chapters one and two, for an account of the events leading up to the establishment of the first Christian communities. Chart the sequence of events.
4. Prepare a report on the life of the apostle Paul.
5. Prepare a report on the Vatican and Vatican City.
6. Look up information on the beginnings of monasticism (the cloistered religious life) in the Christian Church.
7. Try to find out if there are any Protestant or other religious men or religious women in your area. Find out what their specialty is.

4

Protestantism in North America

KNOX
ANGLICAN
baptism
BAPTISTS
GRACE
METHODIST
ISIDOHJJW
CALVINISM
Y.M.C.A.
jan
hus
EPISCOPAL
luther
zwingli

The second largest religious group in North America is the Protestant. The term *Protestant* includes, in popular usage, any Christian or Christian group which is not Roman Catholic or Orthodox. It is an umbrella term which includes several independent, but somewhat related, Christian denominations. There are about ninety-five million Protestants in North America (of about three hundred fifty million worldwide), distributed among two hundred sixty-five denominations.

Protestants, however, do not call themselves Protestants, except insofar as this term means "not Catholic." They refer to themselves by their individual Church identification, such as **Lutheran,** Baptist, **Congregationalist,** Disciples of Christ, and so forth. The term *Protestant,* however, has a third and more important meaning, which tells what Protestantism is. That third meaning is best understood in the context of the history which gave birth to the name.

In 1529 A.D., Charles V, King of Spain and Emperor of what was called the "Holy Roman Empire," called a meeting of the principal rulers of the European states to discuss ways to deal with the ideas and activities of Martin Luther, who was the leading figure in a revolt against the autocratic religious rule of the Pope, and what

Luther considered the religious errors of the Roman Catholic Church.

The meeting was held at Speyer in southwest Germany. A group of five powerful rulers and fourteen powerful city governments refused to accept the findings of the group at Speyer, and that group's solutions to the problems generated by Luther's revolt. The second group published a protest—and the term *Protestant* came into use to signify anyone who protested the declaration of Speyer. By extension, it was applied to people who protested what they felt were the errors and abuses of the "Roman Church."

What Is Protestantism?

Although Protestantism began as a protest against some aspects of Roman Catholic doctrine and practice, it must not be thought of as "against" Roman Catholicism alone. It is a religious movement within Christianity which affirms the witness of the Christian message in its original distinctiveness and purity, unencumbered by institutionalization, a complicated theology, a sacramental system, and an authoritarian priesthood. It stands for the faith of an individual, as distinct from the faith of "a Church."

Protestantism is best understood in the sixteenth century meaning of the word *protest:* to witness or to testify. It is a personal witnessing of faith in Christ as the Savior of the world. It is a proclamation that the world is saved by Christ alone, not by an institution nor by the acts of an institution. It is a positive declaration of convictions which are seen as essential to the Christian faith and message as

preached by Christ and found in the New Testament. It is a way of expressing one's faith in Jesus different from Roman Catholic and Eastern Orthodox expressions.

The Essentials of Protestantism

Because Protestantism, Roman Catholicism, and the Eastern Orthodox Churches are expressions of Christian faith, they agree generally in the essentials of Christian **faith**: faith in Christ, belief in the Trinity, the witness of the New Testament, the meaning of salvation, belief in life after death, the apostolic nature of the primitive Church, Christian love as the basis for morality, and so forth,

Doubtless the most succinct way of setting forth the central teachings of Protestantism is by contrasting them with Roman Catholic dogma; and in an article as brief as the present essay some reliance will have to be placed in that method. By itself, however, it conveys a distorted impression of the character of Protestant faith and practice.

For one thing, this method of contrast misrepresents the experience of the believer. Devout members of Protestant Churches hold the teachings and practices of their Churches precious not because of the challenge they present to Catholicism but because of their efficacy in bringing the faithful worshipper into personal relationship with God. They go to their Churches not to testify against anyone but to receive anew the assurance of the divine mercy.

Christ Church, Philadelphia

Trinity Church, Newport

Again, the method of exposition by contrast ignores the great body of conviction which constitutes the common faith of all Christians, Protestant and Roman Catholic alike. Indeed, so massive is this Christian consensus, and so slight are the differences between Catholics and Protestants by comparison with their agreements in the face of the alternative faiths and anti-faiths now contending for the allegiance of men, that thoughtful members of both groups must be moved to penitence as they consider how little progress is being made toward the reconciliation of these two main bodies of Christian believers.

In the case of Protestant and Roman Catholic, each would affirm vastly more of the other's faith than he would deny. Both believe in the one God, the Creator of the World and the Redeemer of men, who has made known His nature and will and ways through the life, death, and resurrection of Jesus Christ. Both assert man's accountability to this God in response to His requirement of a trustful relationship to Him and a responsible and charitable relationship to one's neighbor.

Even in the much-controverted realm of ecclesiology there is an enormous consensus. In the words of the American Theological Committee's report preparatory to the Lund conference on Faith and Order:

"Every communion holds that the Church is not a human contrivance, but God's gift for the salvation of the world; that the saving acts of God in Christ brought it into being, that it persists in continuity in history by the presence and

81

obscuring the tension between the Church as it is now and the Church as it is destined to become.''

—(World Council of Churches: Faith and Order Commission Papers No. 7, *The Church*) [in] Truman B. Douglass, ''Protestantism,'' *A Handbook of Christian Theology* (Cleveland, Ohio: The World Publishing Company, 1967), pp. 286–288. Reprinted with permission of the publisher.

power of the Holy Spirit. Every communion likewise believes that the Church has a vocation to worship God in his holiness and to proclaim the Gospel to every creature, and that she is equipped by God with the various gifts of the Spirit for the building up of the Body of Christ. And every communion believes that the Church is composed of forgiven sinners, yet through faith already partakes in the eternal life of the Kingdom of God. These agreements cover the Church's origin, the mystery of the Church's present being, and the Church's goal. They ascribe to the Church both a divine and a human element, both a possession and an anticipation of the age to come. They imply an insistence upon the holiness of the Church without any identification of this with a mere human moralism; an insistence upon the visibility of the Church without

Even though Protestantism and Roman Catholicism agree in the essentials of Christianity, they are distinct expressions of Christianity; hence, they differ in many ways: in doctrinal interpretations of certain matters, and on certain religious practices. Although various expressions of Protestant Christianity differ from each other (for example, Lutherans differ from Anglicans and both differ from Baptists), Protestantism differs from Roman Catholicism and Eastern Orthodoxy in several ways. Among the more prominent are:

1. Justification by Faith.
Protestantism usually affirms that people are saved by their act of faith in Jesus—their witnessing that Jesus is their savior—and not by virtue of good works or by the sacraments of any Church. Protestantism does not propose that this is a new article of faith ''invented'' by Protestants. It is, rather, they say, the recovery of what was forgotten, ignored, or seriously downplayed by the medieval Church.

2. Grace Alone Is Sufficient.
Protestantism generally preaches that the act of faith is possible because God acts mercifully in providing the grace necessary for the act of faith. Grace, for Protestants, is God's own action,

apart from rites or ceremonies, and is always available to people.

Sacraments, prayers, good works, and so forth, do not "produce" grace; grace is always present because of who God is and what he does for people's **salvation**. This doctrine is called "the second watchword" of the Reformers. The first is justification by faith alone.

3. The Sinfulness of People.

Protestantism also generally asserts that people are, by nature sinful; that is, they are separated from God and must be reconciled to God by Christ, since they are prone by their undisciplined nature to commit sin.

According to Protestantism, man is always and at the same time both "justified" and a sinner. His life is by nature, in Luther's vivid phrase, "curved in on itself," seeking to find within itself the meaning of existence. . . . Yet God, through the reconciling work of Christ, accepts man as he is. When man by faith acknowledges this acceptance— this "justification"—he is given at least a partial release from this self-obsession and self-idolatry.

—Truman P. Douglass, "Protestantism," *A Handbook of Christian Theology,* (Cleveland, Ohio: The World Publishing Company, 1967), p. 290.

4. The Primacy of the Bible.

Protestantism proclaims that the historical record of Christ's life, death, and resurrection (the New Testament),

along with the Old Testament, set the standards, or norms, for Christian faith, rather than the traditions of men (including the traditions of the Church). Roman Catholics believe also that the New Testament is normative for Christian faith, but that the truth of the scripture is found in the Church, and not in the private interpretation of the individual believer.

> In the Protestant conviction, the Bible becomes true for me through "the inward testimony of the Holy Spirit." . . . the lifeless words of scripture become the living Word when the Spirit illumines the mind of man and convinces him in his heart that God speaks to him, that he acts for him through Jesus Christ.
> —Bernhard W. Anderson, "The Bible," A Handbook of Christian Theology, (Cleveland, Ohio: The World Publishing Company, 1967), page 40.

Protestantism, however, does not limit its contention of the **primacy of the Bible** to the written word. What is of greater importance is what the word proclaims: the reality of Christ. "What is offered in the preaching of the Word is Christ," says J.H. Nichols in his Primer for Protestants. "What is offered in the living of the Word is Christ. What is offered in the Lord's Supper is Christ."

5. The Universal Priesthood of Believers. Protestantism generally asserts that every believer is called to the priesthood in a general sense through baptism. Most Protestant groups recognize the various ministries and that some persons are "called to the ministry," but they deny that there is a special priesthood belonging to some persons through ordination.

Roman Catholic and Eastern Orthodox Churches also affirm the universal priesthood of believers in that through baptism all Christians participate in the Priesthood of Christ. However, these Churches (and some few Protestant groups) also affirm a special priesthood: persons ordained to the sacramental ministry because, they say, Christ selected some special persons to serve special ministerial and jurisdictional function in the Church.

6. The Church. Protestantism thinks of the Church as a fellowship of believers in which every member is a priest, witnessing his faith in common with others in a community of believers such as Lutherans, Episcopalians, Congregationalists, and so forth. It envisions the Church as a broad spiritual union of believers, in contradistinction to Roman Catholics who speak of the Church as "The People of God" gathered into communion with each other forming an institution called the Roman Catholic Church, under the leadership of the Pope, the successor to Peter, the head of the apostles.

7. The Lord's Supper. Protestantism generally has a service recalling or commemorating the Last Supper of Jesus with his close disciples. Individual Protestant groups, however, vary in their understanding of what the Lord's Supper is and means. Many, like the Anglicans and Lutherans, believe in the real, substantial presence of Christ and have a liturgy somewhat like the Roman Catholic Eucharistic Liturgy. Others have what they call a "Communion Service," still others have a commemorative meal, and still others only recall the Lord's Supper in their reading of the scriptures.

8. The Sacraments. Protestantism generally has only two sacraments: Baptism and the Lord's Supper. (Some Protestant groups have other sacraments like Confirmation, Orders, Matrimony, and so forth.) Protestantism does not have a well-defined sacramental theology: some groups believe that Christ acts in the sacraments as he did while on earth; others look on the sacraments only as signs of God's covenant.

Calvin [and those who followed his theology] regarded the sacraments as auxiliary to the Word; what Scripture holds and manifests is afterwards expressed in actions. His aim, therefore, was to maintain a middle course: "A wise moderation should be preserved always and everywhere, not giving up more than is necessary, nor taking away anything that should properly remain." As living images of the Covenant, they are permitted to strengthen our weakness; it is because of this very weakness that we need them, and in making use of them we progress in the life of faith "until he fully unites us with himself in the heavenly life." This is a considerably diminished conception, and it is only by a narrow margin that the sacraments become necessary at all. But we cannot accuse Calvin of directly preparing the way for the disappearance of sacramental practice in the Churches of the Reform. In his view, man's sin and wretchedness is as plain as the denial of all intrinsic value to the sacramental actions; but should Protestantism lose its sense of sin, the sacraments would no longer possess even the importance attributed to them by Calvin. . . .

Since the Word alone gives meaning to the Christian life, Calvinist worship is centred on the Word; God must be heard, and the pulpit assumes a greater importance than the altar which, deprived of its sacrificial significance, becomes a table. Everything is subordinated to the proclamation of Scripture, and preaching, which is the exposition of the Word to the faithful, is central, rather than the Lord's Supper. While the reformed Churches gradually celebrated communion at increasing intervals, they retained the sermon as the centre of Sunday worship. This is true to the logic of the Calvinist reform, although it does not follow its letter; communion is only a kind of secondary preaching of the Word, and if that preaching is frequent then communion must become rarer.

—Georges Tavard, *Understanding Protestantism,* (Glen Rock, New Jersey: Paulist Press, 1964), pp. 32-33.

9. Papal Authority. Protestantism rejects the Roman Catholic claim for papal authority in both the jurisdictional and teaching aspects of the Church. It denies that the Pope has any unique authority in the Church and that he teaches infallibly.

10. Position on the Virgin Mary. Early Protestantism, relying on its fundamental doctrine of justification by faith in Jesus alone, rejected what it considered to be a rather idolatrous "worship" of the Mother of God in medieval Roman Catholicism.

Though Protestants in general recognize Mary as the instrument of Divine intervention in history, they do not accord her any special mediatory place in the relationship between God and people, because "justification by faith alone" precludes any "other" mediators than Christ.

11. Ethical Behavior. Although Protestantism recognizes the primacy of the law of Christian love as the determining factor in moral behavior, it relies more on the individual conscience in making the right choice than do other Christian Churches. Individual Protestants, though relying on their ministers and denominational spokesmen for guidance, make up their own minds on moral issues; they do not depend upon "a Church" to set guidelines for them in determining what is right or wrong *for them.*

Protestantism differs from Roman Catholicism and the Eastern Orthodox Churches in many other ways, but the differences stem from the way Protestantism views the Church, and from its basic doctrines of justification by faith, grace alone, and the primacy of Scripture. In addition, individual Protestant groups differ from each other in their understanding of the meanings of the basic doctrines and how they apply in particular cases. This variety of understanding and of application has given rise to a variety of denominations, each with its own explanations, forms of worship, and religious practices.

The Origins of Protestantism

Protestantism as a religious movement began in Germany in 1517 A.D. when Martin Luther (1483-1546),

Martin Luther (1483-1546)

a Roman Catholic monk, spoke out against what he considered abuses and errors in the preaching of **indulgences** granted to the living and the dead in connection with the drive for donations to renovate St. Peter's Basilica in Rome. It gained momentum when Luther was condemned on various points he raised in connection with debates on the subject, and became a reality when he was **excommunicated** by Pope Leo X (December 25, 1520), and pleaded with the German princes to reform the Church over the heads of the Pope and the bishops. When many of the German leaders sided with Luther and protected him from reprisal, the religious movement called "The Reformation" began.

The Reformation is a term applied to that religious movement which at first challenged the expression of Christianity as practiced by Rome (that is, by the Church under the papacy), then broke from it by organizing Christian communities independent of Rome. The purpose of this separation was to make them more reflective of the image and theology of the Gospels as various reform leaders saw this image and understood the theology of the New Testament. At the same time, Protestantism served the nationalistic aspirations of monarchs who wanted to unify their nations and increase their power.

Various efforts to reform the Church as it was in the latter part of the Middle Ages (approximately 1100 to 1500 A.D.) had been made from time to time. However, it was not until Luther persuaded powerful German princes to side with him in his efforts that any kind of an effective movement to place. At first, it was not a movement

outside the Church. "One should help and cling to the Church," Luther wrote at the beginnings of his attempt at reform. "Conditions will not be improved by separation." It only became separatist when the political, religious, theological, and social forces at work at the time—especially those of a nationalist character—met head-on, and no compromise could be reached. What began as an attempt to reform Christianity in Germany soon spread to other areas, and literally dozens of "reformers" organized their own religious groups in accordance with what they thought the Church of Jesus should be.

The Revolt Spreads

The movement which became known as the Reformation might have been confined to Germany except for the involvement of two other leading personalities of the day: John Calvin

John Calvin (1509–1564)

(1509–1564), a Frenchman who made his religious headquarters in Geneva, and King Henry VIII of England (1491–1547), who became king in 1509 and ruled for thirty-eight years until his death.

If Luther was the prophet of the Reformation, Calvin was its theologian. It was he who forged the theological principles which most influenced developing Protestantism. Calvin was born in France and raised a Catholic, but as a young man he was swept up into the Reformation thinking then sweeping Germany. In 1533 he openly espoused the Protestant cause, and began writing theological essays defending the reform of the Church and advocating much more radical reforms than Luther ever imagined. In 1533 he moved to Geneva in Switzerland, which had become a Reformation stronghold when Ulrich Zwingli (1484–1531), a Catholic priest, persuaded the authorities of Zurich, Switzerland, to adopt the principles of the reform movement. While in Geneva, Calvin wrote his famous *Institutes of the Christian Religion* which became, with Luther's **Augsburg Confession** and his two *Catechisms*, the principal theological works of the Reformation. These became, in effect, the "Bible" of the Protestant movement.

Calvin's principal contribution to the success of the Reformation was his influence on other reformers. His theology was the moving force behind the Presbyterian movement in Scotland and England, and Reformed Churches of Germany, Holland, and Hungary, and the Puritans in England and the United States. It intensified the theology of every Protestant group which arose in the next four hundred

Jonathan Edwards (1703–1758)

years. Calvin's thought influenced even Lutheran and **Anglican** thought which, originally, rejected Calvin's principles.

Calvin's theology was relatively simple. Calvin thought that because God was the Holy Sovereign, only the holy could be saved. But, he taught, because all people are depraved, sinful, and powerless to earn salvation, only those whom God selected for salvation would be saved. All others, Calvin taught, were destined for eternal damnation. This teaching, the heart of what is called **Calvinism**, is known as "the Doctrine of **Predestination.**"*

By the time the doctrine of predestination had been transplanted to 18th-century America, it had taken

---

*Most Protestant groups that follow Calvin's theology have since modified their thinking on the subject of Predestination and the harsher aspects of Calvinistic religion.

on gruesome elaboration. The popular Calvinist preacher, Jonathan Edwards, declared in a sermon in 1741: *"The God that holds you over the pit of hell, much as one holds a spider, or some loathsome insect, over the fire, abhors you and is dreadfully provoked; His wrath toward you burns like fire; He looks upon you as worthy of nothing but to be cast into the fire; He is of purer eyes than to bear to have you in His sight; you are ten thousand times so abominable in His eyes, as the most hateful and venomous serpent is in ours."*—William J. Whalen,

The Religions of the World, (Chicago: Claretian Publications, 1977), p. 12.

King Henry VIII (1491-1547)

According to Calvin, the "elect" had to live as "the elect"—following the sternest restrictions found in the Bible as prescribed by Calvin. In his writing and in his preaching, Calvin stressed the sinfulness of people and the wrath of God ever ready to punish. So forceful and persuasive was Calvin that the people of Geneva begged him to rule their city and set it up as a model of the kingdom of God. For twenty-three years Calvin controlled the religious, civil, political, educational, and social life of the Genevans with an iron hand, punishing severely any person who was caught dancing, drinking, speaking well of the Pope, missing Church, breaking the nine p.m. curfew, or criticizing Calvinist ministers, doctrines, laws, or practice.

What Calvin wanted to do was to restore the Church to what he thought the Bible said it should be. He forbade anything that was not expressly commanded in the Bible; hence he rid the Churches of ritual, art, music, sculpture, stained glass, vestments, ornaments of any kind, and liturgical ceremonies. He spoke against frivolous behavior, even to the point of prohibiting laughter and the play of children in public. In addition to his theological, liturgical, and moral reforms, Calvin also developed a new form of Church government known as the **"presbyterial"** in which the Church was governed by elders, or leaders, chosen by the congregation and not by bishops selected by Church leaders or clerics.

Calvin died in 1564. He left behind a legacy that was unparalleled in the Reformation movement.

The Revolt in England

In spite of what Luther and Calvin did, however, the Reformation

Queen Elizabeth I (1533-1603)

liturgical changes, and took over the affairs of the Church.

The Reformation as we understand the term, however, was not realized in England until the reign of Elizabeth I (1558-1603), Henry's daughter by his second wife, Anne Boleyn, who stabilized the Anglican interpretation of Christianity as the Church of England, and the coming to the throne of William of Orange, during whose reign (1689-1702) the final separation from Rome took place. In between these two periods England was alternately **"Papist"** and "Separated," depending on the current occupant of the throne.

Meanwhile, other dissident groups sprang up in England and Scotland: the Presbyterians, founded by John Knox (1510-1572), a follower of Calvin; the **Methodists,** founded by John Wesley (1703-1791), and the **Puritans**, strict-observance Presbyterians who came into power in England when Oliver Cromwell (1599-1658) was Lord Protector, or chief executive.

After England successfully challenged the authority of Rome in religious matters, the Reformation moved into high gear. Smaller protest movements cropped up everywhere, and protesting groups were formed reflecting the particular Christian expression preached by individual self-styled reformers. In the main, however, the Reformation is identified with Lutheranism in Germany and the Scandinavian countries, Calvinism in Switzerland, Holland, and Scotland, and Anglicanism in England. Almost every Christian group that identifies itself as Protestant reflects the religious philosophy of reform originating in these three areas.

probably would not have succeeded as it did, and certainly would not have been so effective, if it had not been for a third protest against Rome—the one that occurred in England.

Like the reform initiated by Luther, the reformation movement in England began with the protest of one man, King Henry VIII. When Henry failed to obtain authorization from the Pope for a divorce from his wife, Queen Catherine, daughter of the King of Spain, he declared himself head of the Church in England (1534) and demanded that all "loyal" English people acknowledge him, and not the Pope, as the head of the Church in England. He killed off, punished, imprisoned, or banished all who would not accept him as the infallible head of the Church, confiscated Church property, and authorized changes which he felt would make him, in fact, the head of the Church. He appointed bishops loyal to him, authorized

Protestantism Comes to North America

Protestantism might have remained a European phenomenon if it had not been for the discovery of America, and the later missionary efforts of various Protestant groups. Shortly after the Reformation movement began, a rash of religious persecution broke out in Europe and England. Various religious groups fought each other tooth and nail, and the losers were killed, imprisoned, discriminated against, or banished. In some cases, religious groups left their native territory in search of peace and security and a chance to practice their form of Christianity undisturbed. The place most of them came to was North America. The first to come to America to find "their own land" were Puritan Separatists who landed at Plymouth Rock in 1620.

Other groups, of course, had come to North America as missionaries, but the Puritans came, not to convert the Indians, but to settle. Shortly thereafter other groups came to "New England" to settle, bringing their religion with them. Eventually, the east coast of the United States was controlled by English and Dutch Protestantism, and Anglicanism became a dominant religious force in much of Canada when the English defeated the French at Quebec and Canada became part of the "United Kingdom."

Protestantism exercised a profound influence in shaping the cultural, economic, political, and religious destiny of North America through two periods of intense religious activity called the "Great Awakening." The first occurred throughout the colonies, including eastern Canada, between 1730 and 1745. The second occurred

Protestant Communion. *Gari Melchers. Picture Archive.*

Early American Puritans going to church

between 1801 and 1830 and swept
through the southern and western part
of the then United States and the
central portion of Canada. Both may
have resulted from the "New Chosen
People—New Promised Land"
philosophy of Protestant reformers in
England, Scotland, and central Europe.

Many reformers preached—and
political and literary leaders
encouraged—that it was God's will
that Protestant nations or States be
established in which the "true" (that is,
the current) religion be practiced by
everyone in a nation or State, and that
it was the duty of government to
monitor the beliefs, the morality, and
the worship of the citizens to make
sure that the nation or State was God's

kingdom on earth. This philosophy
arose from the conviction that God had
chosen the leaders and the people to
establish a "New Israel" in Europe.

When this philosophy was brought to
the New World, religious leaders took
it as their theme and set about making
the new lands a new "Promised Land"
or "New Zion." They were convinced
that God had sent them to the New
World as his emissaries to make his
promises to Israel come true.
Preachers fanned out all over New
England and eastern Canada preaching
this new doctrine. Through intense
activity and personal contact they
caused a great wave of repentance,
conversion, attachment to the Bible,
and religious enthusiasm to sweep

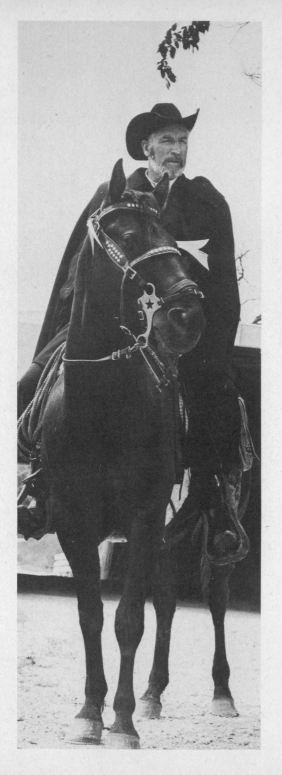

through these areas. Denominational lines became blurred, and a new kind of Protestantism developed—one that was eventually to become distinctly "American."

The first Great Awakening simmered down when the concerns of the American Revolution occupied people's attention. Then, when the United States became a somewhat more respected nation among the political powers of the world after the War of 1812, a new wave of religious enthusiasm occurred. This second Great Awakening, that developed principally in western New York, in the southern and western parts of the new country, and in central Canada, was brought about by **circuit riders,** camp meetings, and revival meetings, which again emphasized repentance, conversion, attachment to the Bible, religious enthusiasm, and the new Promised Land of America. People were swept up into the new awakening, and the religion preached by this new breed of Protestant preacher became an integral part of almost every settlement in the United States and Canada. Like the revival of the previous century, this revival crossed denominational lines, affecting every Protestant denomination except the Anglicans, whose doctrines and forms of worship did not lend themselves to outbursts of religious frenzy.

So successful was the Protestant movement in the United States, that a noted French historian does not hesitate to say that the United States is the leading Protestant country.*

*—Henri Daniel-Rops, *Our Brothers in Christ,* (New York: E.P. Dutton, 1967), page 115.

American Protestantism owes its origins to the Puritans of the seventeenth century who founded the colonies of New England. In search of religious liberty far from Anglican England, they established Protestant states which they attempted to make theocracies in conformity with the "theology of the Covenant." Thus, until 1691, no one had the right to vote in the colony of Massachusetts who was not a recognized member of the Church, and that was a status that could only be attained by the exhibition of satisfactory signs of having experienced inward regeneration, the liberty of divine forgiveness, and conversion of the heart. Citizenship corresponded with divine election; and at most a tenth of the male population, that is, the minority of "visible saints," had voting rights.

Presbyterians and Congregationalists thus settled in New England. The Quakers founded Pennsylvania on principles that opened it up to all religions; Anglicans were established in Virginia. . . . Baptists evangelized the southern States, Georgia, and North Carolina, and soon Methodists settled in Georgia. Methodism spread widely through the Great Revival of 1742 which affected all the colonies and all confessions except the Anglican Church. . . . Later, with the emigrations from Germany, Lutheranism established itself firmly in the region of the Mississippi, from where it was disseminated throughout the continent.

—Georges Tavard, *Understanding Protestantism*, (Glen Rock, New Jersey: Paulist Press, 1959), pp. 95-96.

Once the Protestant Churches were firmly established in Europe (usually as State Churches), they began to send missionaries to the countries into which their governments moved. Because England was the principal world power in the nineteenth century, English Protestantism in its various forms

THE ORIGINAL THIRTEEN COLONIES

sprang up around the world: in India, Africa, Australia, Oceania, Canada, and the United States. It became a religious and moral force in the countries where England dominated. Today, there are over 350 million Protestants practicing their special form of Christianity in almost every country in the world.

Protestantism in North America

Protestantism in North America is expressed in a variety of ways. Its principal characteristic is personal faith in Jesus, but the expression of this faith falls into three broad categories: liberal, conservative, and fundamentalist. Even within denominational confessions, these categories manifest themselves; for example, in Lutheranism, the Lutheran Church in America is considered somewhat liberal, whereas the Lutheran Church-Missouri Synod is considered conservative, if not fundamentalist.

Liberal Protestants are generally considered to be those who accommodate their theology, worship, and ethical responses rather easily to the findings of modern science, philosophy, psychology, anthropology, archaeology, and biblical criticism. They tend to be lenient, receptive to new ideas, openminded, flexible, tolerant, and broadminded in their approach to religious and moral matters.

Conservative Protestants are often thought to be middle-of-the-road,

traditional (without being stuffy), and moderate in their approaches to religious and ethical matters. They are staid in their liturgy, cautious in developing their theology, receptive to biblical discoveries but not uncritical of them, and thoughtful in approaches to modern moral problems.

Fundamentalist Protestants are said to be those who consider certain things in religion to be "fundamental"; that is, essential or unchanging. They reject modern biblical studies (or accommodate them to their views). They especially reject any development in modern learning which seems to threaten their basic view that the Bible is absolutely, totally, and literally (meaning word-for-word what it says) accurate in what it says and how it says it. Fundamentalists insist, for example, that the earth and the firmanent and all living creatures were created exactly as the Bible proposes, that every miracle (for example, Moses' parting the waters of the Nile, God carving the Ten Commandments in stone, and so forth) is factually true, and that the Bible addresses itself to each and every modern problem.

Fundamentalist Protestants are Calvinist in their theology, starkly simple in their worship, generally intolerant of or impatient with other Christians (whom they accuse of deserting fundamental Christianity), strict in their moral stands (which are based, for the most part, on Old Testament moral precepts or stories), and strongly evangelical. They are proud of their adherence to what they consider to be the true faith, and strong in their opinions of what that faith is. Their influence on mainstream North American Protestantism is very strong.

Principal Figures in the Reformation

Martin Luther

1483–1546

Germany

Principal figure in the Reformation and founder of Lutheranism

John Calvin

1509–1564

France

Leader in Swiss reform movement and most influential theologian

King Henry VIII

1491–1547

England

Began reform movement in England

Thomas Cranmer

1489–1556

England

Archbishop of Canterbury and formulator of the principles of the Church of England

George Fox

1624–1691

England

Founder of the Society of Friends (Quakers)

Martin Bucer

1491–1551

Alsace

Reform leader and synthesizer of Protestant doctrine

Ulrich Zwingli
1484–1531
Switzerland

First reformer of the
Church in Switzerland

John Knox
1505–1572
Scotland

Founder of Presbyterianism

John Wesley
1703–1791
England

Founder of Methodism

Menno Simons
1492–1559
Holland

Founder of the Mennonites

Jan Hus
1374–1415
Bohemia

Religious reformer
considered a spiritual
forebear by Protestants

John Wycliff
1320–1384
England

Religious reformer and
translator of Bible.
Considered a spiritual
forebear of Protestantism

Synopsis of Principal Protestant Denominations

African (Methodist) (Episcopal) (Baptist). Congregations of Black Americans who have their own Churches in various Protestant denominations. The term **episcopal** is often included in the Church title to show that bishops head their **hierarchy**, although there may be no ties to the Episcopal Church.

Anabaptist. Anabaptist means "rebaptizer." Anabaptists recognize only adult baptism; they rebaptize converts. They are strict observance Protestants, and fundamentalist in Biblical understanding.

Anglican. The Church which developed from King Henry VIII's revolt against Rome. Generally Protestant in theology but near-Catholic in liturgy. Called "The Church of England" or "The English Church." The Protestant Episcopal Church is the Anglican Church in the United States, which is unaffiliated with the British monarch, who is the head of the Church of England.

Baptist. Baptists are generally fundamentalist Protestants. They accept only adult baptism by immersion. They have simple credal formulas based only on what they think the Bible actually says. They have no sacraments, no priesthood, no bishop or presbyterial rule, and no formal liturgy. The Bible is the sole rule of faith as interpreted by the individual reader. Conservative in doctrine and practice, the Baptists frown on drinking, gambling, card playing, dancing, and the like. Baptists are the largest Protestant group in the United States (one of every three), but are relatively unknown outside North America.

Calvinist. Although there are no denominations which call themselves "Calvinists," the theology of Calvin is the basis of most Protestant denominations. Those that are basically Calvinist in theology tend to be fundamentalist, conservative, simple in their religious services, and energetically evangelical.

68629

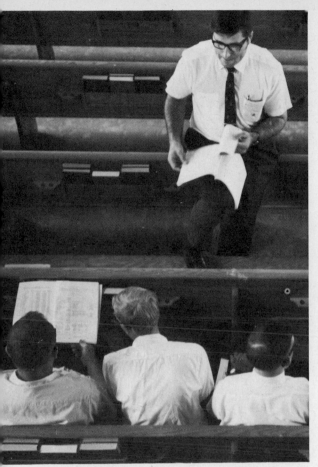

Congregationalist.
Congregationalist comes from the Latin word *congregationes* meaning those who come together in a group. Congregationalists are Protestants of differing origins (but mostly of Presbyterian or Church of England persuasions) who believe that all authority in the Church rests with the local Church or congregation. They differ from their parent Churches in many ways, but principally in their conception of Church authority. Congregationalists are among the most open-minded of the Christian Churches, accepting all who believe in Jesus as the center of their religious life.

"Congregational Christian Churches" is a loose federation of those Christian Churches which have the same fundamental concept of the centrality of the congregation as distinct from those which have authority resting in some person, persons, or group outside of, or distinct from, the individual congregation.

The Disciples of Christ (Christian Church). This group is a union of two separate congregations founded by two different Presbyterian ministers in 1832 who were attempting to restore Gospel simplicity to the Church. One called his group "The Disciples," the other called his "The Christian Church." (The "Disciples" are not to be confused with "The Churches of Christ" or the "Independent Christian Church," which resemble the Disciples in structure, but are conservative in spirit and doctrine.) The only requirement in this Church is belief in Jesus. There are no dogmas, no sacraments, no prescribed liturgy, and no fixed moral positions since private interpretation of the Bible is central to the Disciples Church. The Disciples are organized on three levels: congregational, regional, and general, but each group is totally independent of the others. The worship service of the Disciples is simple: hymn singing, scripture reading, prayer, Holy Communion (which is considered essential to the service), and fellowship. The Disciples of Christ are great promoters of Christian unity.

Evangelical. Originally, the term *Evangelicals* was applied to members of the Church of England who tried to reform the Church more along Gospel lines. Today, very few Churches call themselves

101

Evangelical. The term is used mainly by Churches with strong fundamentalist tendencies, opposed to liberalizing trends within their membership, and by many Baptist, Methodist, and Pentecostal Church groups claiming this quality of zeal in winning souls to Christ. The word is often used as part of the title of some particular Church or other.

Fundamentalist. Like the word *Evangelical,* the word *Fundamentalist* is no longer used to designate a Church group or a sect. It implies, rather, an attitude, state of mind, or approach to religion. Fundamentalists are very strict in their religious and moral practices, accept the Bible as literally true and addressed without qualification to the individual who reads it, and simple in their forms of worship. Many Baptists, and some Presbyterians and Methodists, are Fundamentalist in their religion.

Lutheran. Churches following the principles of Martin Luther. Faith in Christ is the main Lutheran article of faith; with faith in the revealed word of God as found in the Scriptures, especially in the New Testament, following closely thereafter. Lutherans stress a joyful response to God's love as their principal moral imperative. Lutherans have Baptism and the Lord's Supper as their sacraments, with Confirmation, Ordination, and Marriage as sacred rites of the Church. Lutherans are governed by bishops in Europe, but by Presidents in the United States. The Lutherans in the United States are divided generally into three main bodies: The Lutheran Church in America, The Lutheran Church—Missouri Synod, and The American Lutheran Church. Lutherans

United Church of Canada (Presbyterian, Methodist, and Congregational) minister addressing her congregation

are the largest single body of Protestants with about eighty million worldwide, mostly in Germany, the Scandanavian countries, and the United States.

Methodist. In North America, the Methodist Church is now known as the United Methodist Church ever since its merger with the Evangelical United Brethren Church in 1968. The Methodist religion expresses a blend of what its followers believe is New Testament Christianity, the principles of the Reformation, and the thinking of John Wesley, its founder. Methodism is a kind of free-wheeling religion with no formal creed, no formal ritual, and no formal moral code. It stresses simplicity in its approach to all things, with love of God and visible love of neighbor as its chief characteristics. Methodism has two sacraments: Baptism and the Lord's Supper; and two sacred rites: Confirmation and Marriage. About two-thirds of the Methodists live in the United States, where they are known for their extensive social action in the name of the Church.

Pentecostal Churches. Sometimes called "Assemblies of God," these groups, founded by a Welsh miner and a Black Baptist preacher, base their religion on manifestations of the Holy Spirit (the Third Person of the Trinity) through miraculous cures, speaking in tongues, and other charismatic gifts. (They are not to be confused with the modern Pentecostal or Charismatic movements.) Their religion is strictly fundamentalist and their services are starkly simple, with emphasis on fiery preaching, prayer, and declarations of faith and sinfulness, together with repentance. There are often declarations of miraculous cures and miraculous conversions. There are

about eight million members of the Pentecostal Churches, mostly in the United States with a few in Canada and small groups in Mexico.

Presbyterian. Churches which follow Calvin's theology and Church organization (a council of pastors and the laity in a particular Church). The term applies specifically to the Calvinist Church of Scotland and England and their counterparts in the United States and Canada. They have reinterpreted Calvin's doctrine of predestination and have modified, to some extent, his strictures on ornamentation in liturgy and the use of physical symbols in Church. The Church is governed by elected lay people, ministers, and bishops, all with an equal voice. Their influence on Protestantism in the United States far outweighs their numbers in the total Protestant population.

Unitarian. While Unitarians are not considered Protestant by Protestants— nor do they consider themselves as Protestant—they did arise from Protestant sources and do exert influence on much Protestant thinking. Unitarianism is a form of Christianity, but has no dogmatic or moral center in Christianity. Unitarians are rationalists in the narrow sense of the term, relying on their own experiences and their own reason for their religious insights, based on their reading of other religious thinkers (such as Jesus, whom they consider to be simply a "religious genius"). Unitarians include not only those who believe in God, but also those who are atheists, agnostics, secularists, humanists, nature worshippers, pantheists, and secular humanists. Since 1961 the Unitarians have been calling themselves "Unitarian Universalists" because of a merger of the Unitarian and Universalist denominations. Unitarians believed in the unity of all things and that religious preference was incidental to the way one lived (all people can live as one); Universalists believed in the universality of salvation in contradistinction to the predestination belief of the Congregational group from which they separated. The hallmark of a Unitarian Universalist is absolute freedom in what one believes and the acceptance of what others believe.

United Church of Christ. When the Evangelical and Reformed Churches merged with the Congregational Christian Church in 1957, they named themselves the United Church of Christ. The two joined "in order to express the faith of the historic Church expressed in the ancient creeds and reclaimed in the basic insights of the Protestant Reformers." The United Church of Christ has the standard doctrines of Calvinist theology (though modified in light of the times and of the merger) and the worship service of the Congregational and the Reformed Churches, centering around the preaching of the Word and the service of the Sacrament (Holy Communion). Each local Church is autonomous, but all are banded together in associations and in conferences which carry on the work of the Church on national and international levels.

Y.M.C.A./Y.W.C.A. The Young Men's Christian Association and its companion organization, the Young Women's Christian Association are non-denominational organizations interested in the Christian (that is moral) formation of adolescents and young adults by providing them with a place and an atmosphere where they can come together in "guided leisure" to learn to grow to maturity in a Christian way. They are not a denomination or a sect, and they have no dogmas, set moral codes, or forms of worship. The YMCA was organized by George Williams about 1840, in London. It became a formal organization in 1845, and an international organization in 1855. Although it is definitely Christian in its orientation, it is neither a proselytizing nor an evangelical group (pressing this or that belief on members); it welcomes people of all faiths, or none, to share in its endeavors.

For Review and Discussion

1. What does the word *Protestant* mean? What does it signify? How is it expressed in North America?
2. What is meant by the "Reformation"? When did it take place? Who were its principal architects?
3. What was the immediate cause of the Reformation movement? Why did Luther succeed where others failed?
4. What do Protestantism, Roman Catholicism, and the Greek Orthodox Churches have in common?
5. What seem to be the three essential beliefs of Protestantism? Explain each.
6. Name and explain five of the eleven ways mentioned in your book in which Protestantism differs from Roman Catholicism.
7. Why was the discovery of America important to the success of Protestantism? Explain.
8. Make a survey of the Protestant Churches in your area. Give the names, locations, number of members, activities, roots, and whether they seem to be liberal or fundamental in their thrust.
9. Be sure that you can define:

Anabaptist	liturgy
Anglican	Lutheran
baptism	Methodist
Calvinist	Mennonite
doctrine	millenium
dogma	Orthodox Churches
evangelical	papist
excommunication	primacy of the Bible
fundamentalist	presbyterial
indulgence	predestination
justification by faith	Puritan
Lord's Supper	theocracy

For Research

1. Prepare a report on the Holy Roman Empire, especially on its political aspects at the time of the Reformation.
2. Find out what you can about Jan Hus and John Wycliffe.
3. Prepare a brief biographical report on John Calvin.
4. Look up information on the Mennonite sect in North America.
5. Look up some information on the "Great Awakening" in the United States, and its effect on religion in North America.
6. Be prepared to give a historical account of the YMCA and the YWCA. Find out if either of these groups is active in your area.
7. Do some research on the role of Evangeline Booth in the growth of the Salvation Army.

5 The Principal Protestant Denominations in North America

holiness
ELDER
IMMERSION ·
synod
REASON
CRANMER
DENOMINATION
WESLEY ·
holy
club
HYMN
CIRCUIT RIDERS ·
95 THESES ·
SMYTH

If North America—or at least the United States and Canada—is a Protestant continent, as Henri Daniel-Rops contends, it is due not only to the major Protestant denominations such as the Baptist, the Methodist, the Lutheran, and the Presbyterian, but also to the many other denominations which make up the total Protestant world of North America.

At the present time, nine of ten Protestants belong to six denominations or their subgroups: Baptist, Methodist, Lutheran, Presbyterian, Episcopalian, and the Congregational groups. Twenty-one percent are Baptist, eleven percent are Methodist, seven percent are Lutheran, five percent are Presbyterian, and three percent are Episcopalian.

It is impossible in the limited scope of this book to discuss each of the more than two hundred and sixty-five Protestant denominations in North America in detail, and it would really be unnecessary, because most of the lesser known denominations are, as it were, stepchildren of the major groups. It must not be assumed, however, that the subgroups or the "stepchildren"

are not different from the major
denominations. They have differences
in the interpretation of scripture, in
doctrine, in worship, in religious
practices, and in ethical stance. Their
differences, however, are not so great
that they need to be spelled out in this
book. Their similarities to one or
another denomination make it possible
for them to fit into one of the major
denomination discussions. Those that
do not will be discussed in the next
chapter.

The Baptists

One in every three Protestants in
North America is a Baptist. In the
United States they belong to either the
Southern Baptist **Convention** (nearly
12 million members), the National
Baptist Convention, USA (over 6
million members), the National Baptist
Convention of America (nearly 3
million members),* the American
Baptist Churches in the U.S.A. (over
1.5 million members), or to any of the
24 other Baptist groups, such as the
Christian Unity Baptist Convention, the
Duck River Association of Baptists, the
Free Will Baptists, the Two-Seed-in-the-
Spirit Baptists, the General Six-
Principle Baptists, and so forth. Of the
more than 26 million Baptists
worldwide, fully 22.5 million live in the
United States.

In Canada, there are about 450,000
Baptists, belonging chiefly to the
Baptist Convention, the Fellowship
Baptists, and the Regular (Calvinistic)
Baptists. In addition, there are several
smaller Conventions and many

*Both of these are Conventions of Black
Baptist groups.

independent Baptist Churches which do not belong to any association or convention. As in the United States, Canadian Baptists are conservative; they take their cues mostly from the Northern Conventions in the United States. There are some Baptist Churches in Mexico, but their exact number is not known.

The total number of Baptists, or those of Baptist persuasion, however, is not known. Some Baptist groups count only "immersed" believers (those who have been baptized by immersion); some count, in addition to the immersed, those admitted to membership from some other Baptist group; and still others count any who have made a profession of faith with or without baptism. None counts children under the age of twelve.

In addition to the Conventions as such, there is a major difference in the United States between the Southern Baptists and other Baptists. The break between "Southern" and "Northern" Baptists was precipitated some twenty-five years before the Civil War in the United States (about 1840) over the question of slavery. Since that time, opposing views on race, Communion, ecumenism, and the interpretation of scripture have kept the two groups apart. In the main, Southern Baptists tend to be conservative or fundamentalist, and Northern Baptist tend to be more liberal; but individual Baptist Churches may be conservative, fundamental, or liberal wherever they may be.

What Is a Baptist?

A Baptist is a Christian who believes that the Bible is the supreme authority in everything that pertains to religious faith. Because this is the base from

First Baptist Church in America, Providence, Rhode Island, founded 1638 by Roger Williams

which they understand their faith, and because they believe that Luther and Calvin permitted unbiblical elements to remain in their reforms, the original Baptists "purified" the Christian faith by insisting that only adult baptism by immersion is valid; that the Bible is absolutely and literally true in everything it says and that it must be followed exactly;* that scripture speaks to each individual directly without the aid of "interpreters" and that every individual is completely free in religious matters. Because of these premises, Baptists did away with all creeds, sacraments, episcopal or presbyterial modes of Church government, infant baptism, rituals in worship, and religious devotions, all of which, according to Baptist belief, are unscriptural.

Although some Baptists like to trace the Baptist movement to John the Baptist at the time of Christ, most trace their beginnings to English Puritanism and John Smyth (1570?–1612), an Anglican priest who joined the Puritan Separatist** movement. Persecuted in England, Smyth fled to Holland in 1609 where, under the influence of the then-powerful Anabaptist reform, he adopted the belief that adult (that is, "believers") baptism alone is valid. He persuaded some of his fellow exiles to accept this belief as the foundation stone of their Church, and the Baptist movement was born. Although Smyth separated from this group, it continued and became the base for the Baptist movement in North America.

Smyth's group held that any person could be a believer; hence, they became known as "General Baptists." Soon, however, some of his people adopted the strict belief in predestination preached by Calvinists and insisted that only the predestined could be saved. They became known as "Particular Baptists." They then became convinced that baptism by immersion was the only truly scriptural baptism; this doctrine became the accepted mode of baptism for all Baptist Church groups.

After these "Baptists" returned to England, one of their converts was Roger Williams. In order to escape persecution, he went to the Massachusetts Bay Colony in search of religious freedom. Accused of heresy, he was banished from Massachusetts and finally settled in Providence, Rhode Island, where he organized the

Roger Williams (1603–1683)

---

*Many Baptists are no longer strict fundamentalists, but all insist that the Bible is the only authority in faith.

**Separated from The Church of England.

first Baptist Church in 1639. Soon afterwards Williams withdrew from the Baptist Church and creed.

In spite of a shaky start, the Baptist movement flourished in the American Colonies: the General Baptists in the northern tier of colonies; the Particular Baptists in the middle and southern colonies. Spurred by the intense activity of "circuit rider" preachers, the popularity of revivalist approaches, and their passion for religious freedom, the Baptists experienced unprecedented growth, especially in the southern half of the United States, where they remain strong to the present time.

The first Baptist Church in Canada was established in 1763 in New Brunswick by Baptist missionaries from the Massachusetts Colony. Another Baptist Church was established in Nova Scotia about the same time. By 1795, Baptist Churches had been established in Ontario and Quebec, by 1815 in Ottowa and Montreal (by French Huguenots), and by 1873 in western Canada. Canadian Baptists have increased in numbers very slowly, but their percentage in the population has decreased markedly in the last few years because they do not participate in ecumenical activities and because they tend to resist change.

The first Baptist Association was organized in Philadelphia in 1707, and soon several Associations, or as they later became known, Conventions, were formed to strengthen the Baptist movement and coordinate Baptist activities and missions. From these, came the Baptist Conventions in Canada, Mexico, and throughout the world.*

---

*There are, for example, over 500,000 Baptists in Russia, 450,000 in Zaire, Africa, over one million in Asia, 500,000 in South America, and 200,000 in Central America. In all, Baptists are found in one hundred fifteen countries throughout the world.

What Do Baptists Believe?

Because individual Baptist Churches are completely autonomous and individual Baptists are free to believe as they wish, there is a wide range of beliefs and religious practices among Baptists. Some, for example, are fundamentalist; some are progressive. Some belong to the National or World Council of Churches; some do not. Some adhere to a strict, literal interpretation of the Bible; some do not. Some believe in a real heaven and a real hell; some do not. Some have a very strict moral code (for example, no drinking or dancing, no birth control, no abortion, and so forth); and some do not. There are, however, several points of common agreement among Baptists that make them a distinct group within the family of Christian Churches. Among the more important points of agreement are the following:

1. Common Christian Doctrines. Baptists generally believe in the divinity of Christ, the Trinity, salvation through Jesus, immortality, the resurrection of Jesus, and the need to live according to the Christian code.

2. Absolute Authority of the Scriptures. All Baptists agree that the Bible is a complete and absolute guide in all matters of faith and living. They believe that the New Testament is the completely sufficient guide and final authority in all Church matters. They believe that the Holy Spirit guides each individual completely and finally in understanding the scriptures and that each individual is correct in his own interpretation—he may accept guidance, but need not. In any event, he must make up his own mind about what the scriptures say to him. The rallying cry of the Reformation, "*sola* *scriptura*" (the scripture alone), finds its most perfect expression among Baptists.

3. Adult Baptism. Baptists believe that only *believers* (that is, those who can make a completely free affirmation of their faith in Christ on their own) can be baptized. They believe that a person must profess a personal faith in salvation through Jesus, be mature enough to recognize his own sinfulness and experience Christ's forgiveness, and be able to give witness to his faith. They believe that only an adult can do this; hence they do not recognize infant baptism—the baptism of anyone younger than twelve years of age. For this reason, Baptists do not admit that other Christians baptized in infancy are really Christians; hence, most Baptists consider themselves as the only real Christians. They believe in baptism by immersion only, but some Baptists will accept other forms in an emergency.

4. The Concept of Church. Baptists believe in what they call the "gathered Church"; that is, that a Church is a gathering of believers who profess faith in Jesus, are baptized, and come together for worship and fellowship. For Baptists, a "Church" is the local people gathered into a believing community; therefore, there is no supra-organization, or "Church," outside of the local community.

Because of this, Baptists have no hierarchy, no priesthood,* no centralized authority, and no other head than Christ, who is the head of each individual "gathering." No one can tell any gathering or individual Baptist what to believe or what to do:

---

*Baptists do have ordained "ministers of the Word" who are called to serve the local community by preaching and leadership in religious and social matters.

each person and each local community is a complete and all-powerful unit in itself. It may belong to an Association or a Convention to promote local, national, or international Baptist concerns, but need not join any group since it is sufficient unto itself. Although each Baptist congregation is absolutely free and independent, there is a strong feeling of kinship among Baptists: they are mutually supportive of each other in religious, social, and political affairs.

5. Religious Liberty. Because of their strong belief in individual religious freedom, Baptists are strong believers in religious liberty and the separation of Church and state. They resist any attempt by the state or any religious institution to dictate religious matters or controls, and have been the leaders in the fight against anything they believe encroaches on the individual religious liberty of believers. They have spoken out strongly, for example, about prayer in the public schools in the United States, governmental regulations on Churches in Russia and Argentina, and the efforts of various religious groups to, as they say, impose beliefs or moral stances on others.

6. Evangelical and Revivalist Approaches. All Baptists are committed to a strong evangelical and mission spirit. They are ardent, enthusiastic, and zealous in their efforts to win people to faith in Christ in the Baptist mode. They are unabashedly committed to the Gospel and its teachings, to the authority of the New Testament in matters of faith, and to the conviction that salvation is achieved only through a personal and visible conversion to faith in the atonement of Christ.

Because of this, Baptist services tend to be revivalistic. There is emphasis on strong, emotional preaching whose purpose is to awaken, or "revive," the true religious spirit which everyone was supposed to have when he or she originally accepted Christ. Audience response, profession of personal faith, commitment to the tenets of the Gospels, and hymn singing are intended to move the gathering to religious piety and fervor. The purpose of revivalism is not emotionalism in and for itself but to bring back what is sometimes referred to as "that old time religion"—that imaginary golden age of religious awakening.

Religious Practices of the Baptists

Because Baptists are committed to an uncompromising reliance on the literalness of the Bible, and especially of the New Testament, they do not have any religious practice which is not specifically mentioned in the New Testament.

They do not have, for example, any sacraments in the general Christian understanding of the term. Their Baptism is not a sacrament for them; it is an "ordinance"—a prescription ordered by the New Testament. For them, it has no supernatural or sacramental significance. Their Lord's Supper, or communion service, is a reminder of Christ's death only, and is observed either on a monthly or quarterly basis only in obedience to Christ's command "to do this in memory of me." For Baptists, there is

---

*The majority of Christians believe that Jesus is present in the Eucharist.

no "Real Presence,"* no grace conferred or gained, nor any unifying aspect in the communion service. It is strictly a memorial.

Baptists have no feast days (though they do observe Easter, Christmas, and Good Friday), no formulas of prayer (though they do recite the Lord's Prayer), no special devotions, no saints, no shrines, no elaborate liturgies (their wedding ceremonies and funeral services are very simple), and no institutional religious practices. Their common religious practice is to give evidence of their salvation in Christ by faith, good works, and living the Christian ethic as they see it.

The Structure of the Baptist Churches

The Baptists have no formal Church structure. As we have said, they have no hierarchy, no priesthood, no rank, no order of ministries. They do not even refer to themselves as a "Church"; they are a denomination or gathering.

Their Church buildings can be elaborate or simple; their services can be orchestrated or stark; their local Church can be highly organized or loosely administered. The only "structure" the Baptists have is the local gathering which comes to hear the Word (the Bible read and preached) and lives to practice it.

The Methodists

There are about twenty million Methodists in the world over three-fourths of whom live in the United States. They make up the second largest Protestant **denomination** in North America.

The Canadian Methodist Church merged with the Congregationalists and the Presbyterians in Canada in 1925 to form the **United Church of Canada,** and, in 1968, the Methodist Church, U.S.A., merged with the Evangelical United Brethren Church to form the United Methodist Church. What Methodist Churches there are in Mexico are part of the "World Methodist Council" which brings Methodists from all over the world into fellowship and into evangelical and mission efforts.

The Methodist Church has been a strong religious and social force wherever it has been. However, because it is not a "hard and fast" Church with rigid **doctrines,** discipline, forms of worship, or membership, it has found it easy to accommodate itself to other religions, and has sought to merge with other Christian groups of similar beliefs, religious philosophy, approaches to

John Wesley (1703-1791)

religion and living, and concern for social welfare. Methodist mergers with other Christian groups continue, so much so, in fact, that some predict that the Methodist Church as it has been known will no longer exist in the next century.*

What Is a Methodist?

A Methodist is a Christian who subscribes to and follows the religious philosophy of John Wesley, who preached that religion should be "of the heart" (confident of God's love and mercy) and "of the will" (expressed in personal piety and loving concern for one's neighbor). "The Methodist Church," said the late Ralph W. Sockman, a world famous Methodist minister, "is a unique blend of New Testament Christianity, the Protestant

---

*William J. Whalen, *The Religions of the World,* (Chicago: Claretian Publications, 1977) page 22.

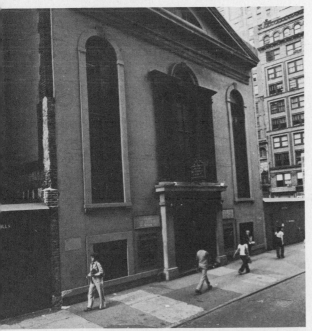

John Street Methodist Church, New York City (1841), mother church of American Methodism

Reformation, and the influence of John Wesley."

The Methodist movement that eventually became the Methodist Church began in England when John Wesley (1703-1791), a devout Anglican priest, convinced that religion ought to have more substance than form, organized societies within the Church of England "in order to pray together, to receive words of exhortation, and to watch over each other in love, that they might help each other to work out their own salvation." At first, Wesley's movement remained in and was an integral part of Anglicanism, but four years after his death, it separated from the Church of England. The breakaway occurred both because Anglican religious authorities refused to recognize the authenticity of Wesley's "special ministers," and because Wesley had preached that Christianity must reflect not only the New Testament and Church traditions but also the experiences of people as they lived their lives, as well as the use of the mind in facing religious questions. To this day, Methodism reflects these four elements in its approach to Christianity: *scripture* (the New Testament, primarily), *tradition* (the theology and worship of the Church of England), *experience* (what is best for people in their particular circumstances), and *reason* (what the mind says is logical and true).

Methodism succeeded in England because of the personal piety and warmth of John Wesley, his brother Charles (who composed over 6000 hymns reflecting the Methodist

---

*Many of these are still used in the Protestant and Catholic Churches of the United States and Canada.

philosophy of religion*), and the ministers who preached Wesley's "way"; because of the preaching ability of these men; because of the substance of their preaching, which stressed God's love and mercy; and because of the openness of Methodist theology, worship, and religious practice. Wesley's religious approach to Christianity was gentle kind, sympathetic, broadminded, and compassionate. Wesley's aim was to have people know, love, and serve God in love, not fear. For Wesley, love of God and love of neighbor were far more important than theology and ritual, though he did not disdain theology and ritual—he subordinated it.

Wesley's movement became known as "Methodism" because of the methodical rules he set down, first for his "Holy Club" at Oxford University when he was a student, and later for his followers. In order to develop personal piety and involvement in charitable endeavors, Wesley set up specific times for prayer (three times a day in public; hourly in private), for reading the scripture and meditation, for visiting the sick poor in England's hospices and forgotten prisoners in jails, and for teaching the children of the poor. His group was laughed at and called "methodists" in derision. The name stuck to his followers and became an honorable and respected title.

Methodism came to North America in the eighteenth century and spread rapidly in the Colonies, especially in the east and south (where one of every three Methodists now live), due primarily to the "horseback ministry" of the many Methodist ministers who packed their saddle bags with the Bible and the Methodist hymnbook, and their

preaching with Wesley's religious philosophy. They went where people were neglected and starved for religious awareness and religious acts. Within a short time there were more Methodists in North America than there were Anglicans, Presbyterians, and Baptists, all of whom had come to North America more than a century before the Methodists began operating in the "New World."

At the present time, in addition to the United Methodist Church in the United States and the United Church of Canada, there are several other Methodist Churches and groups. Among the more well known are the African Methodist Episcopal Church, the African Methodist Episcopal Zion Church, the African Union First Colored Methodist Protestant Church, Inc., (all the foregoing are Black Methodist Churches), the Christian Methodist Episcopal Church, the Evangelical Methodist Church, the First Congregational Methodist Church of U.S.A., the Lumber River Annual Conference of the Holiness Methodist Church, the Primitive Methodist Church, U.S.A., the Southern Methodist Denomination, the United Wesleyan Methodist Church of America, the Reformed Zion Union Apostolic Church, and the Reformed Methodist Union Episcopal Church. In all, there are over 40,000 Methodist Churches in Canada, the United States, and Mexico.

What Do Methodists Believe?

Because Methodism stresses "life rather than creeds," and because there is no central body of dogmatic truths to which Methodists must assent, it is difficult to distinguish Methodism from many of the other major Protestant

denominations. Methodist groups themselves may vary from the belief system of the High Anglican Church to the simple belief systems of many of the Reformed Churches. Methodists are not as fundamentalist as the Baptists nor as theological as the Episcopal or Lutheran Churches. Methodists do, however, accept all of the common beliefs of the Protestant faiths, but give them their own interpretation made in light of developing Methodist theology. They believe in the Trinity, justification by faith, baptism, the Lord's Supper, immortality, the saving actions of Jesus, the centrality of the New Testament, and the law of love as the primary moral imperative.

What makes Methodism different from other Protestant faiths is its belief in the inner experience of religion, and its social application in the real world of experience. At the center of

Methodist belief is what they call the "order of salvation": justification by faith (but not necessarily and exclusively in the righteousness of Jesus), conversion, and sanctification. "Justification by faith," for Methodists, is the acceptance of salvation as a free offering by God through the action of the Holy Spirit. "Conversion" means regeneration and cleansing from a sinful nature through the action of God. "Sanctification," for Methodists, means expressing holiness in a life of prayer and good works addressed to the ethical and social problems of the times.

Methodists believe that they are called to holiness and to social action based on holiness. They are not, however, social activists from a secular or political standpoint; they are social activitists from a religious standpoint. They believe they are called to renew the earth by the command of the New

Testament because all people are children of God.

As far as the Bible is concerned, Methodists believe that it is inspired and "contains all truth required for eternal salvation through faith in Jesus Christ." In keeping with their tradition, Methodists interpret the Bible either liberally or literally, depending on the particular Church and the inclination of the individual. In the main, however, Methodists tend to be rather progressive in their interpretation of the Bible since it is only one of the four guidelines they use in establishing their religious preference.

Religious Practices of the Methodists

Because there are no central doctrinal positions taken by the Methodist Church, there are no common religious pratices among Methodist Churches, even in their understanding, acceptance, and administration of the only two sacraments Methodists in general accept: Baptism and the Lord's Supper.*

For many Methodists, Baptism is a sign of the entrance of a person into the Church. It is viewed by some as a symbolic washing only (by any means); by others it is seen as a grace-ordained and grace-granting ritual in the theological tradition of the Anglican Church. For most Methodists, the

*Most Methodist Churches have confirmation and marriage ceremonies, but they are not considered sacraments because they are not mentioned specifically as such in the New Testament.

Lord's Supper (Holy Communion) is a sacrament of the redemption by Christ's death and a sign of the union of love Christians should have for one another. Most Methodists do not believe in the "Real Presence" in the sense that Roman Catholics or High Anglicans do; they believe that Holy Communion is an expression and symbol of Christ's presence in the community.

Methodists have no devotions, no shrines, no saints, no common prayer formulas (they do, of course, use "The Lord's Prayer"), and no set liturgical or worship rituals. They do gather for worship on Sundays but their worship services vary from Church to Church. The central action in some Churches is the hearing and the preaching of the Word with an invitation to partake in the Lord's Supper. In these Churches the singing of hymns and the profession of faith are important, as is the expression of fellowship. The central action in other Churches is the Eucharistic Liturgy in the manner of the Church of England and the Roman Catholic Church. In these, ritual is solemn and stylized, and the Communion service is solemnized.

For all Methodists, because good works are to be motivated by religion, their good works are religious acts. They are as much a part of their religious practices as are their prayers and worship services.

The Structure of the Methodist Church

Because in Methodist theology all baptized persons are members of the "family of God," there are no ranks or

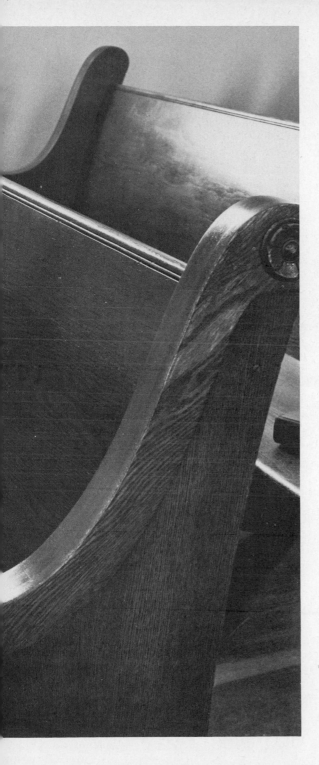

hierarchical structures as such, but there are bishops who preside over an "Area," govern the Church together with clergy and lay people in equal numbers, ordain ministers, and appoint ministers to local Churches. In the United Methodist Church (and some others), women can be, and are, ordained as ministers; they have equal rank with male ministers.

The legislative power of the Methodist Church resides in the General Conference (composed of bishops, clergy, and lay people), and the juridical power resides in a "Juridical Council" chosen by members of the General Conference. The General Conference, composed of delegates from every area in a given segment of the Methodist Church, determines the way the Church is governed and by what laws it shall live. It develops the general principles of Methodism, directs its mission activities, and speaks for the Methodist Churches when the Church feels it is necessary to do so. The Juridical Council sits in judgment on internal affairs of the Methodist Church.

The Methodist Church cooperates fully with Churches of all other persuasions, seeking "the fullness of the mind of Christ [which] can be discovered fully only in a common search, in a common acceptance, in a common active acknowledgement, in common Christian love with all those who call upon the one God to whom we desire to remain open."*

---

*Leo Rosten, ed., *Religions of America,* (New York: Simon and Schuster, 1975), page 184.

The Lutherans

The third largest Protestant denomination in North America is the Lutheran. There are about ten million Lutherans in the United States, three hundred thousand in Canada, and a few in Mexico (perhaps a dozen Churches). Worldwide, there are about seventy-five million Lutherans. Most of the people of Iceland, Sweden, Norway, Denmark, and Finland are Lutherans—Lutheranism is their state Church. Most of the Latvians and Estonians are Lutherans, at least half the Germans are, and there are substantial numbers in most European countries. In recent years, Lutherans have established Churches in Central and South America, in Africa, Asia, Australia, and the Far East. In the United States, Lutheranism is the predominant Protestant Church in the midwest.

The followers of Luther were first called "Lutherans" in a Papal Decree

condemning Luther, and they were so called by their opponents, in derision, in the years immediately following Luther's break from Rome. The name stuck with the Lutherans in spite of Luther's plea that they call themselves "Evangelicals," that is, believers in the Gospel.

Although individual Lutheran Churches are independent and self-governing, most belong to highly organized groups called "**Synods,**" which are officially constituted bodies of Lutheran Churches having the same general approach to Lutheran theology, doctrine, religious practice, seminary training, and policy. The Lutheran Churches in the United States, for example, are divided into twelve synods, the largest of which are the Lutheran Church in America (LCA), the Lutheran Church-Missouri Synod (LC-MS), the American Lutheran Church (ALC), and the Wisconsin Evangelical Lutheran Synod. Ninety-five percent of Lutheran Churches in the United States belong to the first three.

The Lutheran Church in America is the largest of the Lutheran Synods in North America, with over three million members in 6,200 congregations and 7500 ordained ministers. It is considered the most liberal of all the synods, allowing rather broad theological and liturgical latitude to its member Churches. The Lutheran Church-Missouri Synod is the second largest synod in North America with nearly three million members in 6000 congregations and 7000 ordained ministers. It conducts a large parochial school system, second only in size to the Roman Catholic parochial school system. It is considered the most conservative of the three largest synods. The American Lutheran Church is the third largest synod in North America, with about 2.5 million members in 5000 congregations and over 6000 ordained ministers. The Wisconsin Evangelical Synod has nearly 400,000 members in over 900 congregations, with nearly 1000 ordained ministers.

The Lutheran Church in America—Canada Section has 325 Churches and about 125,000 members. The Evangelical Lutheran Church of

Interior, Swedish Lutheran church

Canada, formerly the Canadian District of the American Lutheran Church, has about 320 Churches and 85,000 members. The other Lutheran Churches in Canada are independent or belong to the Lutheran Church—Canada, which is the Canadian branch of the Lutheran Church-Missouri Synod.

What Is a Lutheran?

A Lutheran is a Christian who subscribes to and follows Martin Luther's interpretation of what Christianity is as this interpretation is expressed in the "Augsburg Confession."*

Lutheranism began when Luther posted Ninety-five Theses on the door of the castle Church at Wittenberg, Germany, on October 31, 1517.** As we mentioned on page 88, Luther objected to what became known as "the sale of indulgences" and proposed a debate on the subject by posting his "Ninety-five Theses." These were his reasons for opposing the exaggerated claims for indulgences made by a Dominican friar (a member of a religious order of men), Johann Tetzel, who was granting "certificates of

---

*The Augsburg Confession (or formal profession of belief) is a statement of belief and doctrine as formulated by Philip Melancthon (1497–1560), Luther's associate and theologian. It was presented at the Diet (Conference) of Augsburg, Germany, in 1530, and became the principal statement of belief, or creed, of all Lutheran Churches.

**A thesis is a statement, or proposition, proposed for discussion or debate. Posting notices on Church doors was a common practice in medieval Europe. The Church door was a kind of community bulletin board.

indulgence" to any who would contribute money to the fund for the restoration of St. Peter's Basilica in Rome.

What began as a proposal for debate, developed into a Church-wide confrontation when letters of praise for Luther's position poured in from all over Europe. As time went on, what had begun as a protest about indulgences, spread to other aspects of doctrine and practice as expressed in the medieval Church, and became, in effect, a power struggle involving the authority of the papacy. (It is important to note that Luther did not say he was right and the Church was wrong when he began his protest. He simply wanted to debate, or to have serious discussions, on the points he raised.) What had begun as a "minor disturbance by an obscure monk of no importance," soon engulfed the whole medieval Church and led to Luther's condemnation and excommunication.

Luther was ordered to appear before Charles V, Emperor of the **Holy Roman Empire,** at the **Diet of Worms** (in West Germany) in 1521. He was told to withdraw his objections and renounce his actions (he had publicly burned a copy of Church law in defiance of the Pope) or be punished. In a reply that has since become a rallying cry of Protestantism and Luther's most remembered saying, he said: "I neither can nor will recant anything, since it is neither right nor safe to act against conscience. Here I take my stand. I cannot do otherwise. So help me God." With that, he left the congress to face arrest and punishment by Charles' men. Instead, he was rescued by the German princes who supported his movement and given asylum in a castle in Wartburg,

Martin Luther (1483-1546)

the Roman Catholic Church. It was the meshing of Luther's own theological position with the Church's inability to curb its worst practices that created the schism in Christian ranks between Protestant and Catholic.

—David Wallechinsky & Irving Wallace, *The People's Almanac* (Garden City, New York: Doubleday and Company, 1975), page 494. Reprinted by permission of Doubleday & Company, Inc.

Luther's objection to the indulgence-preaching by Johann Tetzel stemmed from his own deeply personal and internal struggle for the meaning of salvation. He had accepted what had become standard theological preaching in the medieval Church—that salvation must be earned by good works—but, realizing his own sinfulness (Luther was a good, pious, sincere, and learned monk), he worried about his own personal salvation, fearing he would not be saved because of his sins. Almost in despair, he searched the New Testament for the answer to justification (freedom from sin and its penalties). When he read: "I am not ashamed of the gospel. It is the power of God leading everyone who believes in it to salvation, the Jew first, then the Greek. For in the gospel is revealed the justice of God which begins and ends with faith; as the Scripture says, 'The just man shall live by faith' " (The Epistle of Paul to the Romans, 1:16-17) he was suddenly enlightened and relieved. He had found his answer: *it was not by a person's own efforts but by the grace of God that anyone is saved.* (This became the basis for the slogan "justification by faith" that is a keystone of Protestant Christianity.) From that moment on, Luther taught

where he began his translation of the Bible into German (the official Bible was in Latin) and the codification of his beliefs. This work and his subsequent "Catechisms" became the basis for the Lutheran expression of Christianity.

It must be remembered that Luther did not intend to start a new Church; he only wanted to reform the Church he loved.

Martin Luther was, in fact, a reformer; he was not a revolutionary. He was an insider, a member of the establishment, who for personal and psychological reasons—as well as out of concern for his fellow Christians—could not remain silent in the face of what he considered to be gross impiety on the part of

and preached his theological position on salvation. Needless to say, when Johann Tetzel preached his brand of indulgence theology in Wittenberg, Luther opposed him. The rest is history.

Luther's revolt spread like wildfire in northern and eastern Germany and to the Scandinavian countries, where Lutheranism became the state religion. (It had limited success in other European countries.) It came to North American in 1624 when Dutch merchants settled in "New Amsterdam" (later New York City on Manhattan Island). By 1638, Lutheran Churches flourished on the east coast of the United States. The Churches adopted the presbyterial form of government and organized synods to form a united Lutheran movement. In the general immigration period after the War of 1812, when German and Scandinavian people came to the New World, Lutheranism became a dominant force in American life, especially in the middle west of the United States where these immigrants settled in force. For years, Lutheranism was the predominant religion in the midwestern states of the United States.

What Lutherans Believe

Although the Lutheran reform movement was precipitated by the differences Luther had with the theology of indulgences as it was preached in 1517, its roots eventually went much deeper than that. As time went on in the initial struggles, Lutheranism opposed other aspects of doctrine and religious practice as these were expressed in medieval Roman Catholicism. Two main points of opposition were Luther's doctrine of justification by faith alone, and the

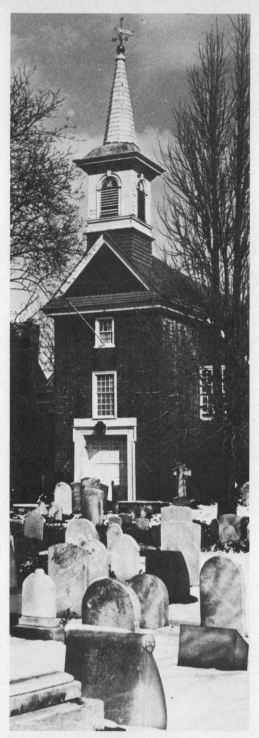

Old Swedes' Church, Philadelphia

question of where final authority in the Christian Church resided.

As far as justification is concerned, Roman Catholicism seemed to stress good works; Lutheranism insisted that faith was the means to justification. Roman Catholicism said that final authority in the Church resided in the papacy, which had absolute authority in matters pertaining to doctrine, morals, and worship; Lutheranism said it resided in the scriptures. Roman Catholicism judged the Church by its loyalty to the Pope; Lutheranism judged the Church by its loyalty to the scriptures. From these two, other differences developed, and, as time went on, Lutheranism, instead of being a reform of the Church from within, developed into a separate Church group expressing its view of Christianity in ways which made it different from and separated from both Roman Catholicism and the Eastern Orthodox Churches.

As it developed, Lutheranism remained the most traditional of the European Reformation Churches. Unlike other Protestant movements, Lutheranism retained in both its doctrine and religious practices those things in Roman Catholicism which it believed were not opposed to scripture. More radical Protestant groups did away with everything not expressly mentioned in the scripture. This difference remains to the present day.

Lutherans believe, for example, all the articles in the traditional Christian creeds—the Apostles' Creed, the Nicene Creed, and the **Athanasian Creed.** They believe in the Trinity, Christ's divinity, the Incarnation, eternal life, the forgiveness of sin, the efficacy of God's grace, baptism, the necessity of liturgical form in worship, the Lord's Supper, the free gift of salvation in Christ, the reality of sin, and so forth.

Lutherans don't claim any doctrines different from the common Christian faith described in the Apostles' Creed. We are created by God, but we employ the freedom given us by God to disobey our Creator. The result is continual tragedy in human life. But God did not abandon us in our tragedy. He shares it with us.

In Christ, He reveals Himself as the Savior God, suffering punishment and death so we may share with Him in the resurrection from death. Through faith in Christ, a new life begins in us. It is nourished by God's gifts through His Word and sacraments. The Word is recorded in the Bible, but the Word itself is a living, active thing through which the Holy Spirit stirs us to growth in understanding and obedience to God's will.

—G. Elson Ruff, "What Is a Lutheran?" *Religions of America,* (New York: Simon and Schuster, 1975) pages 158-159.

Lutherans, however, believe that only two of the traditional sacraments are scripture-ordained: Baptism and the Lord's Supper. Baptism, they believe is the beginning of the life of faith—through Baptism a person is born into the Kingdom of God. The Lord's Supper, they believe, is an encounter with the Living (resurrected) Lord, who is truly present in Holy Communion to forgive sins and renew the faith-life of the believers. Some Lutherans receive Holy Communion once a month; others, weekly. They partake of both the bread and the wine.

Other sacraments of Christian tradition—Confirmation, Marriage, and Orders—are, for Lutherans, rites of the Church only. They have no special grace nor special merit. Penance is not generally recognized in Lutheran Churches (though some do have a "confessional rite") because, they believe, sins are forgiven directly by God of all who ask forgiveness. The Anointing of the Sick is only a pious Christian action; it is believed to be therapeutic only.

Most Lutherans view Confirmation as the highlight of their religious life. The young Lutheran is admitted to Confirmation at the age of 13 or 14 only after a thorough study of the catechism. In a Lutheran parochial school, this means a study of Christian doctrine during the seventh and eighth grades; a Lutheran attending the public school might spend several hours a week for a year to prepare for Confirmation.

The rite itself includes an examination on Christian doctrine, an intercessory prayer by the congregation, and the laying on of hands by the pastor. The service is usually scheduled for Pentecost or Palm Sunday as part of the worship service. As he blesses each confirmand, the pastor recites a verse from the Bible which takes on a special, lifelong meaning for the Lutheran. This same verse is often woven into the wedding service and even the funeral eulogy.

Generally Confirmation is a prerequisite for admission to the

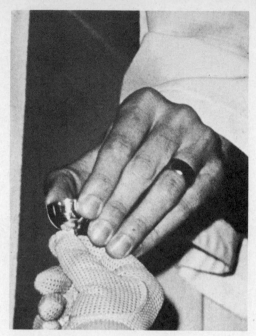

Lutheran Communion Service

Lord's Supper, although some Lutheran Churches now allow young people to receive Communion before Confirmation. Those Churches which do allow this belong to the Lutheran Church of America or the American Lutheran Church rather than the Missouri or Wisconsin Synods, which maintain the older tradition.
—William J. Whalen, *U.S. Catholic,* October 1978, p. 38. (Reprinted by permission of *U.S. Catholic* / Claretian Publications, 221 W. Madison, Chicago, Illinois 60606.)

Lutherans place a great deal of emphasis on faith, because they believe that Christian living is a result of true Christian believing. That is why the Lutheran Church trains its ministers so thoroughly (ministers, however, have no special rank or claim no special grace of office), conduct intensive learning programs for all members of a congregation, have a parochial school system, and why they still conduct "heresy trials" for pastors and others suspected of deviant doctrinal positions.*

Religious Practices of the Lutherans

The principal religious act of Lutherans is their Sunday worship service. The typical service includes a confession of sin, a declaration of salvation by God's grace, an entry psalm, or song, the recitation or singing of the traditional "hymn of praise," and the official prayer of the congregation. This is followed by the Bible readings, the recitation of the creed, a Lutheran hymn, and a sermon on the Bible readings by the minister. The Bible readings and the sermon are the highlights of the typical Lutheran Sunday service. When the sermon is finished, the congregation joins in a prayer service, makes an offering, sings more hymns, and receives a blessing invoked by the minister. On "Communion Sundays," the service includes the consecration ceremony of the bread and the wine (recalling the Lord's Supper from the New Testament accounts), and the reception of the bread and wine, usually while kneeling at the altar railing. In many Lutheran Churches, the Sunday service is followed by a period of "fellowship" when members of the congregation meet with each other and their pastor.

Lutherans do not have any special religious devotional services, cult of the saints, or shrines of pilgrimages, though some may take privately sponsored trips to the Holy Land. They do observe the major Christian feastdays like Christmas, Easter, and Pentecost and follow the traditional Church

Installation of a Lutheran minister

Calendar of Seasons: Advent (before Christmas), Christmas, Lent (before Easter), Easter, and Pentecost.

Because there is no "official" liturgical form that all Lutheran Churches must follow, there is a wide variety in Lutheran worship services. These may range from the elaborate "Rome-like" liturgies of Lutheran cathedrals where a bishop presides at the service, to the simple service of a typical small, rural pastorate such as might be found almost anywhere in the United States, Canada, and northern Europe.

The Structure of the Lutheran Church

The Lutheran Church in Europe is governed by bishops in countries where the Lutheran Church is tied traditionally to State governments. In North America, however, the Lutheran Church has a more democratic form of government. Presidents, or bishops, are elected for a limited time, and their authority is restricted. In all Lutheran Churches, the foundation of authority is in the individual congregation where "the free people of God exercise their right to hear the Word and receive the sacraments." They do not recognize any hierarchical authority in matters of faith.

Nevertheless, there is a kind of moral unity in the Lutheran Church. Lutherans are bound together in various synods for practical and operational purposes, but also to preserve unity in what they call "the essentials of doctrine and scripture." Any individual Lutheran Church, however, may leave one synod and join another if it feels that its synod does not represent the religious feelings of the congregation.

Lutheran ministers have no special rank and no special authority in the Lutheran Church, but they are given a reverence of honor because of their calling and their special ordination. "The authority of the clergy," says Conrad Bergendoff, an authority on Lutheranism, "derives from no constitutional organization, but from the proclamation of a gospel and the administration of sacraments in accord with scriptural revelation."[*]

The Presbyterians

The fourth largest Protestant group in North America is the Presbyterian. There are about 8 million Presbyterians in the United States and 168,500 in Canada, among about 20 million world-wide. Presbyterianism is the Established Church of Scotland. The English monarch is the head of the Church when present in Scotland.

Presbyterians are found throughout the world. There are at least 4 million in the Netherlands, 1.5 million in Communist Hungary, 600,000 in Rumania, 400,000 in Czechoslovakia, and lesser, but substantial, numbers in Australia, Oceania, New Zealand, and the countries of South America. In the United States there are ten different Presbyterian groups, the largest of which is the United Presbyterian Church in the U.S.A. In Canada, the Presbyterians joined with the Congregational and Methodist Churches to form the United Church of Canada.

---

[*] *A Handbook of Christian Theology,* (Cleveland: The World Publishing Company, 1967), page 221.

Presbyterianism is part of the larger Protestant movement known collectively as "the Reformed Churches" which resulted from the Reformation movement in Switzerland, Holland, France, Germany, Hungary, England, and Scotland. Most Presbyterian Churches in North America are offshoots of Scottish and English Presbyterianism and follow the essential aspects of the doctrinal, liturgical, and constitutional findings of the Westminster Confession of faith approved in 1652 by the English Parliament. It is this confession of faith which makes Presbyterianism different from other Protestant groups in general and other Reformed Churches in particular.

What Is a Presbyterian?

A Presbyterian in North America is a Christian who accepts and follows the Reformation theology of John Calvin (see pages 88-90) as it was preached by John Knox in Scotland and later adapted and modified by succeeding Presbyterian leaders. Essentially, a Presbyterian is one who belongs to that expression of Christianity which views the Church

> *as a body of people who have been, who are now being, and who yet shall be . . . reconciled to God and their fellow-men in Jesus Christ. Being bound together in a common reconciliation, the believers are in fellowship, or communion, with Christ and with each other on the basis of God's grace and forgiveness given to each and to all.*
>
> —Leonard J. Trinterud, "Presbyterianism," *A Handbook of Christian Theology*, (Cleveland: The World Publishing Company, 1967), page 274.

John Knox (1505-1572)

The name "Presbyterian" comes from the Greek word *presbyteros,* meaning "elder," and refers to the philosophy and form of Church government found in this expression of Christianity. Each Presbyterian Church is governed by "elders": *teaching* elders who are ordained ministers or pastors charged with preaching the gospel, instructing the faithful, and administering the sacraments; and *ruling* elders who are elected from the ranks of the Church. In each Church the elders form a "session" with final and supreme authority in all spiritual matters in a local Church. In addition, each Church has a board of deacons who administer the works of charity of the Church and a board of trustees who hold the property in the name of the Church and see to its upkeep.

Presbyterianism began in Scotland when John Knox (1505–1572), a fiery, charismatic preacher brought the theology and Church organizational plan of John Calvin to Scotland from Geneva, Switzerland, where he had gone seeking refuge from persecution. At first, Presbyterianism was a movement within the Church of England—part of the Puritan movement. Eventually it became a separate Church when Cromwell's Puritan party was ousted from power.

Presbyterianism came to North America early in the seventeenth century when members of the Dutch Reformed Church settled in New Amsterdam (New York) and the Puritans settled in New England. The Dutch Reformed group eventually joined the Congregationalist Church (now the United Church of Christ) and the Puritans joined the various Presbyterian groups in New England.

The Presbyterians were mostly Scots and Scotch-Irish (Scots who had settled on land in Ireland seized by the King of England from Irish landowners) who settled mostly in New York, New Jersey, Pennsylvania, Maryland, and Delaware, though some spread from New England to Georgia. Presbyterians arrived by the thousands after 1710 and became the most influential Church group in the rebellion of the Colonies (called "the Presbyterian rebellion" in the English House of Commons). At least fourteen signers of the Declaration of Independence were Presbyterians.

With the westward movement in the United States, Presbyterianism spread rapidly. It split into groups, most notably into the Northern and Southern synods during the Civil War. In recent years, various mergers of Presbyterian groups have taken place, and more are envisioned.

Western Presbyterian Synod

St. John's Church, Richmond, Virginia, in which Patrick Henry made his "Give me liberty" speech, March 23, 1775.

In Canada, Presbyterianism took root after 1763 when Irish Presbyterians from New Hampshire in the colonies settled in Nova Scotia and large numbers of Scottish Presbyterians settled there in 1773. From there it spread westward, and in 1875, all Presbyterian Churches formed the Presbyterian Church in Canada. In 1925, as we said, the Presbyterian Church in Canada joined with the Methodists and the Congregationalists to form the United Church of Canada. (Some Presbyterians refused the merger and continue to call themselves the Presbyterian Church in Canada.) The United Church of Canada is essentially Presbyterian in government, but in doctrine and religious practice, both the Methodists and the Congregationalists have retained most of their own traditions.

The Presbyterian Church in the United States and Canada is not the same Church theologically that Calvin and Knox envisioned. It has remained "**presbyterial**," but it has become much more liberal in doctrine and religious practice than either Calvin or Knox would have tolerated.

What Do Presbyterians Believe?

Presbyterianism did not spring up as a new Church or as a separated Church. It sprang up as a reform of the Church based on Calvin's view of what the Church should be, according to his understanding of it from his reading of the New Testament,

especially the Gospels and St. Paul's epistles. That is why Presbyterianism is structured and organized as it is.

The Reformation Churches (and all of the Protestant groups based on them) developed, basically, from the view of the Church held by the three principal reformers. Lutheranism developed from Luther's view; Anglicanism developed from Cranmer's view (he had been appointed archbishop of Canterbury by King Henry VIII, who declared himself head of the Church of England); and the Reformed Churches developed from Calvin's view. Presbyterianism is one of the Reformed Churches.

Presbyterianism moved away from some aspects of Calvin's view of the Church (accommodated to the political needs in England and Scotland where it began and developed) and later rejected or reinterpreted his doctrine of predestination. Today it retains little of its Calvinistic beginnings, except in small Church groups, and resembles most liberal Protestant Churches in doctrine and religious services, fitting in somewhere between Lutheranism and Methodism.

Like other Protestant groups, Presbyterians believe that justification, or salvation, is accomplished in Christ. Unlike many Protestant groups, however, Presbyterians believe that justification takes place only in the Church, which is God's means for justification in Christ. "One can be reconciled to God only as he is also reconciled to his fellow-men," says Leonard J. Trinterud; "hence the biblical metaphor of being brought into the presence of God only by becoming a member of a body of which Christ is the head."

The Christian life, the new life in Christ within the Church, is not its own end. This world is the creation of God, and continues in existence despite its rebellion and failure because of God's determination to fulfill, in mercy, His creative purpose and will. Reconciliation to God in Christ means, therefore, reconciliation to God's will and purpose for mankind as disclosed in Jesus Christ. That this will and purpose are truly made known in Jesus Christ leads to the conviction that order and law are given by God as means to responsible common life among men. The structure of society and the form of law and justice are to be shaped, as nearly as may be possible by civil means, to the will and purpose of God in Christ. The Church and the State, however, are not one, but rather two distinct entities separate in nature, in function, and in administration. (Here Presbyterian theory and practice often conflicted in British history.)

The service of God is not the doing of something for the benefit of God, but the service of obedience to God. Ecclesiastical, ritual, or liturgical acts are therefore only contributing factors to the service of God. The social, political, economic, etc., aspects of human life are as "sacred" as that which is usually termed "the sacred." Rather than a "secular" realm, accordingly, over against a "sacred" realm, there is only an unreconciled realm over against a reconciled realm. The "secular" belongs to God, and has a role to play in the "sacred" purpose of God. To that purpose, or to God who thus purposes for it, the "secular" needs to be reconciled.

The Christian life, the Christian vocation, the religious life devoted to Christ, or life in the fellowship of Christ among his people the Church—all these are synonymous—cannot be equated with any "clergy," or professional religious leadership or group. The Christian vocation is a calling to live in Christ through the Church in every aspect and phase of human life. The areas of human life to which God may call a Christian are as diverse as the extent of God's creative and redemptive intention in Christ. Wherever the Christian is, it is his vocation to bring that part of God's creation into a reconciling fellowship with God which embraces and reconciles also one's fellow man.

—Leonard J. Trinterud, "Presbyterianism," *A Handbook of Christian Theology* (Cleveland: World Publishing Company, 1967), pages 274-5.

In other things, modern Presbyterians believe as other Christians do in what are called the essentials of Christianity with, of course, their own interpretations and explanations. They believe in the Trinity, the divinity of Christ, the incarnation, the resurrection, the Bible as revelation ("the only infallible rule in faith and practice"), eternal life, the reality of sin, the need for forgiveness, the law of love as the guiding principle in morality, the need for community worship service, and in two sacraments only: baptism and the Lord's Supper.

American Presbyterians, however, do not believe that baptism is necessary for salvation, nor in the physical presence of Christ in Holy Communion. For them, baptism is only a sign of God's covenant, and so it is important only as a ceremony of entrance into the Church. The Lord's Supper is only a commemoration of the sacrifice of Christ, and Christ is only spiritually present in the bread and the wine. It is a common-participation sacrament in which the entire Church is brought into fellowship with Christ; it brings them into the presence of God.

Religious Practices of Presbyterians

For Presbyterians, worship is not something done for God, or even simply to worship him. It is part of God's total work in redeeming the world through his Son, Jesus. For them, God reveals himself in all things, but particularly in his "Word"—his communication of himself in Baptism, the Lord's Supper, the scriptures, preaching, and community prayer. For this reason, the Sunday worship service combines these elements.

A typical worship service includes the call to worship, prayers, hymns, hearing the word of God in Bible readings and in preaching, prayers for the Church, and the "going forth" ceremony of blessings and dismissal. When the Lord's Supper is included (eight times per year), it comes after the preaching.

In addition to the Sunday worship service, Presbyterians have confirmation, marriage, burial, and ordination services for its ministers. These are not sacraments for Presbyterians; they are acts of the Church with no particular sacramental significance.

In all their ceremonies, Presbyterians now employ rich and elaborate

symbolism—a departure from the original Presbyterian practice. Their services are now relatively solemn, and their rituals elaborate. Where once they had simple rooms or plain Churches, they now have Church buildings on the medieval plan, and they use candles, vestments, the cross, decorations, and well-trained choirs.

Presbyterians do not have shrines, special devotions, a cult of the saints, or religious feasts, aside from the major Christian feasts of Christmas, Easter, and Pentecost, and the traditional seasons of the Church year.

The Structure of the Presbyterian Church

The Presbyterian Church in North America is governed by a democratic form of representative government, with officers elected by the Church membership. Half of the electors must be lay people. There is no order of rank in the Presbyterian Church, and there is no permanent hierarchy.

In addition to the "sessions" spoken of above, the Presbyterian Church has what it calls "**Presbyteries**" composed of ministers and elders from several congregations in an area. The presbytery ordains ministers (both men and women) and conducts Church business in a particular area. When ministers and elders from several presbyteries convene for Church business, it is called a "synod." Once a year, the representatives from all presbyteries and synods gather in what is called a "General Assembly." This is the final court or highest authority in the Church in all matters pertaining to the entire Presbyterian Church. In all these assemblies, lay people are eligible for, and are often elected to, the highest office, called "moderator."

The Presbyterian Church in North America may not now be the Church of John Calvin or John Knox, but Presbyterians attempt to be faithful to the idea of these reformers: reflecting the Church of Jesus Christ as they see it in light of the circumstances in which they find themselves.

The Anglicans/ The Episcopalians

The fourth largest Christian denomination in the world is the Church of England with some 60 million members, half of whom live in the British Isles.* It is generally called "The Anglican Church" in every country except the United States and Scotland, where it is known as "The Protestant Episcopal Church." There are about 4 million Episcopalians in the United States and about 1 million Anglicans in Canada.

It is called the Protestant Episcopal Church, or simply the Episcopal Church, in the United States because in 1783 the Anglican Church in the newly formed United States chose the name Protestant Episcopal Church to designate its separation from allegiance to the king of England, who is the head of the Church of England. It chose the word "Protestant" to signify that it was not Roman Catholic (it looked like Roman Catholicism in many ways), and the word "episcopal" to designate its system of government, which was episcopal rather than presbyterian or congregational—the forms of government used in most Protestant Church groups.

Although at the present time the distinctions within the Anglican/ Episcopal Church are minimal, there are three "kinds" of Anglicanism, called "high," "low," and "broad." The "high" Churches emphasize the

King Edward VI (1537-1553)

Catholic tradition of solemnity in services; the "low" Churches emphasize simplicity in services and give greater emphasis to the Biblical aspects of their services; the "broad" Churches are either high or low in worship services, emphasizing a liberal approach to Christian traditions and values.

At the present time within the Anglican/Episcopal Church there is also a movement called "**Anglo-Catholic.**" It is a movement seeking to restore all Roman Catholic doctrinal and liturgical approaches, excepting only the primacy of the Pope.

The Anglican Church is sometimes called "the bridge Church," for it spans the gap between Protestantism in its European expressions and Roman Catholicism. Members believe that it expresses the spirit of Protestantism within the Roman Catholic tradition.

---

*The first three are Roman Catholic, Eastern Orthodox, and Lutheran.

Thomas Cranmer (1489–1556)

What Is an Anglican/ Episcopalian?

Anglicans in Canada and Episcopalians in the United States are members of the worldwide Anglican communion, observing the same forms of worship, most of the doctrines, and many of the religious practices of the Church of England.

The original Church of England is the mother Church of all Anglican Churches, and the Archbishop of Canterbury (the ecclesiastical center of England) holds the primacy of honor among all Anglican bishops. All Anglicans are in communion with each other and with the Church of England, and the **Book of Common Prayer** and the *Thirty-nine Articles of Religion* establish the doctrinal, liturgical, and spiritual practices of all Anglicans. More than any other Protestant

Church, the Church of England is a unified body of Christians expressing the same general doctrinal and liturgical approaches to Christianity.

The Church of England, as we said, resulted from a dispute between King Henry VIII and Pope Clement VII about a divorce Henry wanted from his wife, Queen Catherine. As time went on and he failed to achieve his goal, Henry declared himself head of the Church in England. In 1532 he appointed Thomas Cranmer Archbishop of Canterbury. It was Cranmer who engineered the separation and set the tone for the Reformation in England. In 1534, at the urging of Cranmer, Henry demanded that all English clergy sign The Act of Submission, which declared that he was, in fact, the real head of the Church in England. In 1535 Pope Paul III excommunicated Henry, and Henry began dismantling the power of Rome in England. He suppressed monasteries, deposed, deported, or executed bishops and priests who refused to acknowledge him as head of the Church, confiscated Church lands, and outlawed the Roman Church.

In spite of his anger and his actions, Henry insisted on maintaining all Roman Catholic doctrines and practices—his anger being directed against the Pope who, he insisted, had too much to say about English affairs.* That is why the Church of England

---

*The dispute over the divorce was only the occasion of the split between the Church in England and the Church of Rome. The cause was a five-hundred-year-old dispute over what the English considered unwarranted and unnecessary incursions into the affairs of England by the Popes in Rome. The dispute was, in its final analysis, not religious, but political.

maintains most of the doctrines and traditions of the Roman Catholic Church.

The real character of Anglicanism was not forged until the reigns of Henry's son, King Edward VI (1547-1553), who commanded that *The Book of Common Prayer* (the worship service book) be used in all Churches in the kingdom, and of Elizabeth I (1558-1603), who commanded that the *Thirty-nine Articles of Religion* (the thirty-nine points of essential doctrine of the Church of England) be adopted as the creed of all English Churches. For the next eighty-five years, the Church in England was alternately "English" or "papist." During the reign of William of Orange (1689-1702), the separation was finalized, and "papists" were outlawed until the Catholic Emancipation act of 1829 was passed.

The Anglican Church came to North America with English explorers. The first Anglican settlement was in Jamestown, Virginia, in 1607, which became "an Anglican colony." Soon there were Anglican Churches in the southern counties of New York, in Maryland, Georgia, and the Carolinas. All were attached to the mother Church in England until after the Revolutionary War, when Samuel

Glebe House, Woodbury, Connecticut, where Samuel Seabury was sworn in as first Episcopal bishop of the United States.

Seabury was consecrated the first Anglican bishop in North America. He was made bishop of Connecticut. Anglicanism first settled in Canada in the seventeenth century (in Nova Scotia) and it, too, was attached to the mother Church in England until 1787, when the first bishop was consecrated in Nova Scotia. It soon spread west and became the dominant Protestant Church group in Canada. Today there are twenty-eight Anglican dioceses and four provinces in Canada.

What Do Anglicans/ Episcopalians Believe?

Because of the nature of the Reformation movement in England, the reformers retained almost all of the doctrinal, liturgical, and religious traditions of the Western Church. They changed only the language used in worship and the administration of the sacraments, put more emphasis on the Bible as a source of interpretation of dogma, and rejected the authority of the Pope in English Church affairs.

Over the course of the years, the English Church moved away from other things found in Roman Catholicism, due chiefly to interpretations and explanations of these matters, and did not accept many of the things Roman Catholicism legislated into its doctrinal, liturgical, and moral positions. In the main, however, Anglicanism/Episcopalianism is the most traditional expression of Christianity of all the religious movements that sprang up in Europe at the end of the Middle Ages.

The Anglicans/Episcopalians accept all of the traditional Christian doctrines spelled out or implied in the Apostles' Creed and the Nicene Creed. They

Anglican candidates for ordination greeting the congregation

believe in the Trinity, the divinity of Christ, the incarnation, the virgin birth, the resurrection, the inspiration of scripture, the salvational aspects of Christ's life and death, eternal life, the primacy of love as the basic moral imperative for Christians, and the sacramental nature of the traditional seven sacraments of Christianity.*

Unlike most Protestant Churches, the Anglicans/Episcopalians believe in the real presence of the Body and Blood of Christ in Holy Communion; in the hierarchical nature of the priesthood (bishops, priests, deacons); in the apostolic succession of the office of bishop;** in the invocation of the saints; and in the religious, or monastic, way of life. (There are communities of Anglican priests and nuns throughout the world who take vows of poverty, chastity, and obedience.)

Individual Anglican/Episcopal Churches, or regional bodies, may differ from others in some aspects of belief, but, in general, worldwide Anglicanism displays a remarkable unity in its understanding and expression of Christian faith.

---

*Baptism, Confirmation, the Eucharist, Penance, Orders, Matrimony, and the Anointing of the Sick.

**The uninterrupted line of succession from the time of the apostles.

Religious Practices of Anglicans/Episcopalians

The philosophy, nature, and order of Anglican/Episcopal religious services are spelled out in the *Book of Common Prayer* which, as we said above, is the worship service book used by all Churches associated in the Anglican Communion. This book, first used in 1549, contains the order of service for the Holy Eucharist, the Morning and Evening Prayer services, the Litany, and the season services for the traditional Church seasons of Advent, Christmas, Lent, Easter, and Pentecost. Although it has been revised many times to meet changing needs, its principle of ordered worship as the most fitting way to worship God has been retained.

In keeping with this tradition, Anglican/Episcopal religious services are solemn, official acts of the Church. Church buildings may be large or small, medieval or modern in style, but they are always pointed to liturgical use. Candles, incense, holy water, rich vestments, sacred vessels, and music play important roles in many religious services in the Anglican/Episcopal Churches, whether these are official liturgical acts or pious practices of individual Churches.

Holy Communion, sometimes called the Lord's Supper or the Holy Eucharist (and recently, sometimes, the Liturgy of the Eucharist or the Eucharistic Liturgy), is the principal service of worship in the Anglican/Episcopal Church. It resembles the Roman Catholic Mass in its purpose, intent, and general order, and is always a solemn community action full of rich symbolism and ordered ritual. There is an entry service of prayers and hymns, a Biblical service of selected Scripture readings, an Offertory ceremony, a Consecration service in which the bread and the wine are consecrated, the recitation of the Lord's Prayer, Holy Communion, and the dismissal service. All of these flow into one another to form one continuous service leading up to or following the Consecration and Communion, which are the principal actions of the Anglican/Episcopal Lord's Supper.

In all Anglican/Episcopal Churches the sacraments are solemnized and ritualized, and play an important part in every Church member's life. Morning and Evening prayer services are an official act of the Church. In

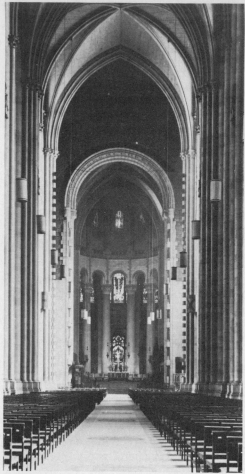
Cathedral of St. John the Divine, New York City

The Structure of the Anglican/Episcopal Church

Although the Anglican/Episcopal Church has no universal supreme authority, it does have an ordered hierarchy and a system of government that controls individual Churches or areas and attempts to keep the Church faithful to the traditions of the Church of England.

A bishop is a head of a diocese (area of the Church) and looks out for the spiritual, liturgical, and doctrinal aspects of a diocese. He also ordains priests (or ministers as they are sometimes called), appoints them to parishes, and looks after the religious orders or monasteries in his area.

A priest, or "rector" as the pastor of a parish is called, a Church warden (a lay person who looks after the secular affairs of a parish), and an elected group of lay people govern a parish. (Many episcopal Churches have two wardens—senior and junior, or rector's and people's. They have separate functions in some parishes.) A "convention" of clergy and elected lay people make decisions affecting a diocese, and a National Convention consisting of two "houses," or groups, governs a national Church. In England, the ruling monarch is the nominal head of the Church of England, and the English Parliament must, in theory, approve all actions of the Church of England. Most of the time this approval is automatic and perfunctory, or routine.

All Anglican/Episcopal Churches look to the office of the Archbishop of Canterbury as the spiritual leader of the Church, but he has no real authority over the independent conventions of National Conventions of the Churches in union with the

many Churches Benediction of the Blessed Sacrament (the Eucharist) is held regularly; in some, devotions in honor of the Blessed Virgin are encouraged; and in all, the traditional saints are venerated.

Individual Anglican/Episcopal Churches have other religious practices suited to the needs and desires of the individual Churches. All Anglican/ Episcopal Churches put great emphasis on prayer, devotion to a personal Christ, and the work of the Holy Spirit in the life of the individual and of the Church.

Anglican Communion.* Every five or ten years (more often if necessary), the Archbishop of Canterbury invites representatives of all the Anglican/ Episcopal Churches to a meeting in London to discuss Church policy. Whatever decisions are arrived at, however, do not bind individual Churches; each is responsible for its own affairs.

The Anglican Church has had a great influence on the spiritual and moral life of the world because of its leadership in the political, economic, and cultural life of the countries belonging to the British Empire or Commonwealth of Nations. The influence of Britain as a nation is waning, but the influence of Anglicanism is still strong.

Other Protestant Groups in North America

Roman Catholics, Baptists, Methodists, Lutherans, Presbyterians, and Episcopalians make up about three-fourths of the religious population of North America. The rest are either "other Protestant," Jewish, Mormon, or belong to any number of

---

*For example, the 1978 National Convention in England voted not to admit women to the priesthood, even though the Archbishop of Canterbury had urged them to do so. In the United States, the General Convention of the Episcopal Church voted to ordain women to the priesthood when it met in 1976. There are now a number of women serving as priests in parishes, institutions, and colleges.

Principal Beliefs and Practices of the Majo

Denomina-tions	Credal Formulas	BELIEF IN:		Eternal Life	Sacraments
		Trinity	Divinity of Christ		
Anglican/ Episcopal	Apostle's Creed. Nicene Creed. Book of Common Prayer. 39 Articles of Religion.	Yes	Yes	Yes—states of being. Union or alienation.	Seven sacrame
Baptist	No official creed or statement of belief.	Some do; some do not	Yes	Some believe in literal heaven and hell. Most believe in some kind of existence after death	Adult Baptism
Lutheran	Apostles' Creed. Nicene Creed. Athanasian Creed. Augsburg Confession. Formula of Concord.	Yes	Yes	Yes. Kingdom of God realized in next life only.	Baptism. Lord's Supper.
Methodist	No formal creed. Book of discipline. Hymnbook.	Yes	Yes	Indefinite. Most believe in a realm of mind and spirit in an afterlife.	Baptism. Holy Communion. Confirmation is act of church as introduction to a status.
Presbyterian	Apostles' Creed. Nicene Creed. Westminster Confession.	Yes	Yes	Some accept heaven and hell; some don't. All accept some form of life after death.	Baptism. Holy Communion.

rotestant Denominations in North America

Worship Service	Biblical Authority	Church Government	Saints
emn Eucharistic Liturgy, yers, hymns, Bible dings, sermon, nmunion. Morning and ning prayers.	Bible is source of Christian doctrine. Church interpretation and tradition give authority to Bible.	Episcopal by areas. United morally to Archbishop of Canterbury. No central infallible authority.	Yes
e service: hymns, fession of faith, prayers, dings, preaching. nmunion once a month as norial service only.	Absolute private interpretation. Bible is final and only authority. Some accept literal and some liberal interpretation.	Independent churches. Local church is sovereign all-powerful unit. Local minister is teacher.	No
e service: hymns, yers, readings, sermon. d's Supper or Holy nmunion.	Final authority in matters of faith and life. Gospels and Paul are principal texts used.	Within individual congregation, bishops or presidents elected with limited authority. United in synods.	Some, of ancient tradition.
eral service: prayer, dings, hymns, sermon, wship. Occasional Lord's per.	Bible contains all truth for salvation.	Democratic. Equal clergy and lay government. Independent churches. Loose union. Some bishops.	No
nal service: call to ship, prayers, Bible dings, sermon, hymns. asional Lord's Supper.	Bible alone is infallible rule of faith and practice. Literal or liberal interpretation.	Each congregation rules church through elected representatives.	No

independent religious groups or Churches that cannot properly be classified as "other Protestant," and certainly are not Roman Catholic, Jewish, or Mormon.

Of the "other Protestant" Churches, the most well-known are the Disciples of Christ, the United Church of Christ, and the Congregationalist Churches. Each of these expresses a form of Christianity that is a variation on the theme of one of the major Protestant groups mentioned in this chapter.

These and other Protestant groups were discussed briefly on pages 100–104.

It is important to understand that even though these "other Protestants" are not associated with the larger Protestant groups, each plays an important role in the lives of the people who belong to them. In them they find the kind of religious faith and practice that suits their religious needs as they attempt to express a relationship with what God is for them.

For Review and Discussion

1. Prepare a statement about each of the major Protestant religions that would distinguish it from the others. Discuss your statements with your classmates and come up with some final statements to make the distinctions clear to whoever might inquire about the differences.

2. Be able to relate the origins of each of the major Protestant religions. If you are a member of another Protestant religion than those mentioned, prepare a statement about the origin of your own.

3. Be prepared to say how each of the major Protestant Churches got started in North America.
4. What seems to be the reason for the growth of the Baptist and Methodist Churches in the United States?
5. Why do most Protestant Churches have only two sacraments? What do they mean by a sacrament?
6. What triggered Luther's revolt against Rome? What was his position in the matter? Why was Luther's revolt successful?
7. Describe the structure of each of the major Protestant Churches.
8. Select one of the beliefs or practices from one of the religions discussed thus far (other than your own, if any) which you would find difficult to accept. Be prepared to discuss your difficulty in an open forum.
9. Be sure that you can define the following:

Anabaptist	episcopal
Anglican	hierarchy
Anglo-Catholic	literal interpretation
Augsburg Confession	minister
Book of Common Prayer	Ninety-five theses
creed	presbyterial
circuit rider	sacrament
Diet	synod

For Research

1. Prepare a brief report on the life of Martin Luther.
2. Prepare a brief report on the controversy involving Henry VIII and the Papacy. Find out why the reigning monarch of England has the title "Defender of the Faith."
3. If you can, attend a religious service of a Church to which you do not belong. Report on what takes place and how it affects you.
4. Select one of the major Protestant groups in your area. Find out when that group began services in your area. Select one of the "other Protestant" groups in your area. Find out about its beginnings.
5. Find out the names of three hymns by Charles Wesley. What is the theme of each? What famous hymn did Martin Luther write?
6. If you are not a member of one of the major Protestant Churches, prepare a brief report on the origin, principal beliefs, and major religious practices of your own Church, if you belong to one.
7. Find out the origin of the following place names: Nova Scotia, Newfoundland, New England, New Jersey, Virginia, Maryland, Vera Cruz, Quebec, Montreal, Pennsylvania, New York, Puerto Rico, New Orleans, Louisiana, Georgia, Santa Fe, San Francisco, Florida, Cuernavaca, California, Arizona, and British Columbia.

6

Other Influential Religious Groups in North America

MORMONS
AMISH
JACOB
seder
icon
QUAKERS
TALMUD
torah
law
jew
HANNUKAH
JUDEA
nauvoo
HEBREW
moses
RABBI

There are many other Church groups that play important roles in shaping the religious and moral tone of North America besides Roman Catholicism and the Protestant Church groups. Among the more widely known are the Jewish people, the Eastern Orthodox Churches, the Mormons, the Seventh-Day Adventists, the **Christian Scientists**, the **Jehovah's Witnesses**, and the Quakers.

The Mormons, the Seventh-Day Adventists, the Christian Scientists, the Jehovah Witnesses, and the Quakers are not Protestants in the general understanding of the word *Protestant*, even though in many ways they "look like" particular forms of Protestantism. They do not consider themselves Protestants; each thinks of itself as "another way" of expressing a relationship to God. They are "Christian" in the sense that they accept Jesus, but they are not Christian in the way Roman Catholics, Eastern Orthodox Christians, or standard Protestants are.

Judaism, of course, is the religion from which Christianity sprang, and the Eastern Orthodox Churches form the largest Christian group outside of the Roman Catholic Church.* There are over 14 million Jews in the world, and more than 123 million members of the Eastern Orthodox Churches.

The Jews

Over 6 million of the world's fourteen million Jews live in North America—twice as many as live in the State of Israel. There are nearly 6 million in the United States, over 275,000 in Canada, and a few in Mexico, mostly in Mexico City and Acapulco.

The names *Jew* and *Judaism* come from *Judaeus,* the Latinized form of the word *Yehudi,* meaning "descendant of Judah" in Hebrew. The "descendants of Judah" were the Jews living in Judea, the southern portion of the original "kingdom of Israel" whose capital was Jerusalem. It was called "Judea" or the "Kingdom of Judah" because that portion of Palestine was given to the tribe of Judah (and the tribe of Benjamin) when the Israelites conquered Canaan (modern Palestine) after their escape from slavery in Egypt about 1280 B.C. The tribe of Judah was one of the twelve tribes of Israel, each tribe named after one of the sons of Jacob who was the second son of Isaac, the son of Abraham, the "Father of the Jewish people."

---

*There are, of course, more Protestants than Eastern Orthodox but they do not form a single Church group as the Eastern Orthodox Churches do.

Orthodox Jewish pilgrim prays at the Western Wall, Jerusalem

Prophet Abraham Visiting His Wife, Sarah. *Post Safavi period, first half of 18th century. Free Library of Philadelphia / PICTURE ARCHIVE.*

Although the term *Jew* is often used interchangeably with *Israelite* and *Hebrew* in modern communication and conversation, it has a rather precise meaning in Jewish history and literature. In Jewish history, a *Jew* is anyone of the Jewish religion or heritage who has lived since the return of the Jewish people from exile in Babylon to Jerusalem in 538 B.C. An *Israelite* is one who was a member of one of the tribes who escaped from Egypt and was covenanted to God in the desert and formed part of the Kingdom of Israel from about 1200 B.C. to 587 B.C., when Jerusalem was destroyed and the leaders of the Jewish people were taken as prisoners to Babylon.* A *Hebrew* is one of the descendants of Abraham who lived in what is now Palestine and wound up in Egypt about 1300 B.C.

For the purposes of discussion in this book, the terms *Jew* and *Judaism* refers to the Jewish people and their religion as it is today.

What Is a Jew?

A Jew is any person who traces his spiritual heritage to a group of people who were led out of slavery in Egypt by Moses, one of the foremost religious leaders of all time. A person may be a Jew by his religion—one who accepts the faith of Judaism and practices it. A person might be a cultural Jew—one who accepts the heritage and the folkways of Judaism as his heritage and folkways. A person might be a sociological Jew—one who considers himself a Jew whether he practices his religion or not and who is considered a Jew by the Jewish people.

"A Jew," says Morris N. Kertzer, a prominent **rabbi**, "shares a common history, common prayer, a vast literature, and, above all, a common moral and spiritual purpose. Judaism is, really, a way of life."** According to Professor Mordecai Kaplan, Judaism is "a civilization."

A Jew is a person committed to Judaism in one way or another. He or she shares in a common religious heritage, an outlook on life that is specifically Jewish, a Jewish way of living, and a Jewish commitment to a people that stems from a tradition of a God-directed, miraculous deliverance from evil experienced by his or her ancestors over three thousand years ago.

Judaism traces its origins to a man named Abraham, who left his homeland in Haran (on the border of modern Turkey and Syria) at what he believed to be the direction of God, and settled in Canaan. Jewish tradition tells us that God promised Abraham a land he could call his own and that his descendants would become a great nation (Genesis 12:1–3). The Jewish Bible tells us that Abraham was faithful to his God, that he and his descendants prospered, and that his sons, grandsons, and great-grandsons carried on the traditions of Abraham: faithfulness to their God. It is from this tradition that the Jews refer to their God as "the God of Abraham, of Isaac, and of Jacob."

As we said above, the descendants of Abraham wound up in slavery in Egypt. Jewish tradition tells us that

---

*In modern times, Jews who are citizens of the State of Israel are called "Israelis" to distinguish them from other Jews.

**Religions of America*, page 143.

they were brought out of Egypt by God under the leadership of Moses. While they were working their way back to "the land of Abraham" through the Arabian desert, they were formed into a religious nation when Moses pledged that they would be faithful to their God (called, from this time on.
"**Yahweh**"*), and would observe all the commandments that their God would give them. (This is the occasion of the reception of the famous "Ten Commandments" of Jewish and Christian tradition.)

There [the people of Israel] set up camp at the foot of Mount Sinai, and Moses went up the mountain to meet with God.

The Lord called to him from the mountain and told him to say to the Israelites, Jacob's descendants: "You saw what I, the Lord, did to the Egyptians and how I carried you as an eagle carries her young on her wings, and brought you here to me. Now, if you will obey me and keep my covenant, you will be my own people. The whole earth is mine, but you will be my chosen people, a people dedicated to me alone, and you will serve me as priests." So Moses went down and called the leaders of the people together and told them everything that the Lord had commanded him. Then all the people answered together, "We will do everything that the Lord has said," and Moses reported this to the Lord.

—Exodus 19: 2–8

*Meaning "I am," or "I am who am," or "My name is 'I am'." The word *Jehovah,* in English comes from another form of this word for God: *Yehowah.*

This incident describes the key event in Jewish history, and is the point of departure of the religious faith and the religious practices of the Jewish people. From that time to the present, the Jewish people have struggled valiantly and successfully, many times at seemingly insurmountable odds, to preserve their existence, their identity, their religion, and their way of life.

Jews came to North America as early as the first voyage of Columbus, but they did not settle until much later. By 1621 there were Spanish Jews in Virginia; by 1649 there were Jews in Massachusetts; and by 1658 there

were Jews in Maryland. It was not until 1654, however, that a group of Jews, fleeing persecution in Brazil, settled as a group in New York. It is from this date that Jewish historians mark the date of real Jewish history in the United States.

From 1650 to about 1825, the Jewish population was about 10,000 in the United States. From 1825 to 1880, the Jewish population increased to about 25,000 because of the political turmoil in Europe. From 1880 to 1920, two million Jews, mostly from Russia, settled in the United States. Just before and just after the Second World War, thousands of Jews fled to the United States from Nazi Germany and the difficulties in Europe.

Jewish immigration to Canada developed slowly, much as it did in the early years of the United States—by individuals and not by groups. As a group, members of the Jewish faith in Canada have not attained the prominence or power that many Jews have in the United States. What Jews there are in Mexico have little influence as a group on the national economic, political, or cultural life.

Kinds of Judaism

Judaism can be expressed in three different ways: Orthodox, Conservative, or Reform.

Orthodox Jews, who like to be called "Traditional," are those who observe the Torah* in both its scriptural and traditional expressions in a strict way. They observe the letter of the Law regarding the **Sabbath**: they do no work, do not travel, write, or conduct business, and they do not carry money or light fires. They observe the dietary laws to the most minute detail,** they separate men and women in the **synagogue**, and use

---

*The Torah can mean two things. Its first and principal meaning is the first five books of the Jewish Bible: Genesis, Exodus, Leviticus, Numbers, and Deuteronomy. In a broader sense it means the entire body of Jewish law as it is contained in scripture and tradition.

**Orthodox Jews do not eat meat from a pig or a horse, or any kind of shellfish. The meat they eat must come from an animal that has hoven hoofs and chews its cud (for example, a goat, sheep, cow, or deer), and must be slaughtered in a certain way (kosher). Meat products and dairy products may not be eaten together.

Touro Synagogue, Newport, Rhode Island (1763)

only Hebrew in their prayers and ceremonial services. The men wear a hat or a skullcap (called a *yarmulke,* which the most pious wear at all times) and often have beards. Many of them sway back and forth during prayer, simulating the movement of a rider on a camel, in memory of the days Jews were forbidden to ride camels in Palestine.

Conservative Jews observe the pattern of traditional Judaism, but adapt it to circumstances of time and place. They observe the Sabbath, the festivals, and the high holidays, but may use the vernacular as well as Hebrew. They adapt services to the needs of the community as it is in a particular time and place. They observe the dietary laws with minor changes. The men wear hats or skullcaps only during religious services. Conservative Jews look on themselves as middle-of-the-road.

Reform, or Liberal, **Jews** accept only the ethical laws of the Torah as binding, and observe only a few of the religious practices of ancient Judaism. They do not follow any customs not compatible with modern civilization (believing, for example, that many of the dietary laws were commanded for health reason and not for moral reasons), do not separate the sexes in the synagogue or temple, and may use the vernacular in all religious services. They allow instrumental music in their synagogues, and permit modern expressions of ancient rituals They stress a liberal interpretation of the Bible and the **Talmud**.

Both Conservative and Reform Jews are moving more and more toward traditional practices, reintroducing some customs abandoned as irrelevant, in order to be more closely identified as Jews before the world.

All three groups, in spite of their differences, share a common faith: the oneness of their God and the need to bear witness *as a people,* to the commands of their God for the good of all people. There is an awakened awareness among the Jews of their traditional concept of themselves as "the chosen people." They do not think of themselves this way in pride. It is, rather, an obligation they take on: they believe that they have been selected by their God to make him and his ways known to all, that they have been "chosen" to carry the message of his word. It is, they believe, a heavy, but joyful burden. Serious Jews of whatever persuasion try to make their faith a reality.

What Do Jews Believe?

Jews do not have a creed in the commonly accepted definition of the term. They do, however, have sacred writings which contain their beliefs and their laws. It is these writings and these laws which make Judaism what it is, because the writings spell out for them who and what their God is and what is his will. Their laws make every action, sacred or secular, a religious action because it is done in conformity to God's expressed will as it is given in the sacred writings.

The principal sacred writing of the Jews is the **Torah**—the first five books of the Jewish Bible, sometimes called the **Pentateuch** or "The Law of Moses." Second in importance is the Talmud, a collection of laws, commentaries on the law, traditions, sayings, poetry, stories, biographies, and prophecies of ancient Jewish tradition.* In addition to the Pentateuch, the Jewish Bible also contains the Psalms, the Prophecies, and the Writings. The Psalms are sacred songs or poetry; the Prophecies are the collected words of Israel's prophets, or leaders; the Writings are all the other materials considered biblical but not contained in the Pentateuch or the Prophets. All of these materials are sacred to the Jews, but only the Pentateuch is "The Law," or "Torah."

The principal Jewish belief spelled out in the Bible, and proclaimed in

Jewish Law and practice, is the oneness, omnipotence, and glory of God. This may not seem so distinctive in light of what Christians and Moslems believe, but when the Jews proclaimed this startling concept of God, it was. The people among whom the Hebrews, then the Israelites, lived, believed in many gods, and had the power and the will to assert that their gods were right. In opposition to, and in defiance of, all others at the time, the Jews proclaimed that Yahweh was the One God. The Jewish proclamation then as now, was: "Hear, O Israel, the Lord is our God, the Lord alone!" (Deuteronomy 6:4).

The Jewish concept of God, however, did not simply encompass the idea of oneness, omnipotence, and glory. It meant also that God was

---

*The Talmud was preserved at first by word of mouth and later in written form. There are two Talmud: the Jerusalem Talmud and the Babylonian Talmud. Jewish practice today follows primarily the Babylonian tradition.

Conservative rabbi dressing the Torah

transcendant, **immanent**, merciful, just, kind, and loving. It meant that God cared for people and was intent on making them what they were created to become: his people, created in his image.

Because of what they believe about God, the second major belief of the Jews is that all people are equal in God's sight. For the Jews, each person, regardless of his station in life, is special because he belongs to God. Therefore, the Jews believe, if God cares for each individual, so must the community care. For the Jews, this is God's will: it must be done. This accounts for the emphasis among the Jews on caring for their own, and for the fierce loyalty of many Jews for all things Jewish: economic, social, political, and cultural. What seems to stem from national or racial pride is, in reality, a matter of religious faith. The Jews believe that they are God's "own people . . . a people dedicated to me alone, and you will serve me as priests" and that they must act the part and be a holy nation: like God, caring for his own.

The Jewish awareness of who and what God is gives rise to a third important belief of the Jews: God must be worshipped. One of the principal acts of worship is the observance of the Sabbath (the seventh day of the week) from sunset Friday to sunset Saturday. Whether a person is an Orthodox, Conservative, or Reform Jew, the Sabbath is important: it is a holy day. Services are held in the synagogue or temple where the Torah is read, studied, and explained, and where prayers and sermons may be part of the observance. The Sabbath is a "home day"; it is observed in the home by the family through ritual and prayer.

Lighting the Sabbath candles

The Jewish people have been referred to as the "people of the Sabbath." The makers of the Talmud considered the observance of the Sabbath as the very foundation of the Jewish faith. . . .

It has been said that "More than Israel has kept the Sabbath, it is the Sabbath that has kept Israel," and this statement is hardly an exaggeration, because the Sabbath has received so much emphasis through the centuries that all other days find their meaning in this one day. . . .

The Sabbath officially starts at sundown on Friday and ends at sundown on Saturday. Normally, the mother lights two candles shortly before the beginning of the Sabbath, concluding with the blessing: "Blessed art Thou, O Lord, our God, King of the universe, who has

sanctified us with His command-
ments, and commanded us to kin-
dle the Sabbath light.'' She then
usually adds another prayer for the
members of her household.

When the father—with or with-
out his family—returns from the
synagogue, the evening meal is
ready to begin. The father blesses
the wine, the two loaves of twisted
white bread called ''hallah'' which
are invariably a part of the meal,
and the children. There is a meal
after the synagogue service on Sat-
urday morning and an important
meal to bring the Sabbath to a
close. At the latter there is not only
a benediction of the wine but a
blessing of spices kept in a special
box for the occasion. Often a spe-
cial twisted candle is lit at the con-
clusion of the Sabbath, as a farewell
to the ''princess'' until the next
week.

—Lee A. Belford, *Introduction to Ju-*
daism, (New York: Association
Press, 1961). Reprinted by permission of Follett Publishing Company.

A fourth concern, amounting in
effect to a belief among Jewish people,
is love of learning. Believing that the
way to know God and to do his will lies
in knowing who God is and what his
will is for them, the Jewish people put
great stress on knowing the Bible.
Jewish children attend Hebrew classes
faithfully, primarily to know the Bible,
and adults read the Bible faithfully and
study the traditions of the great rabbis
to know what the Jewish way of life
really is for them. This emphasis on
learning spills over into general
education where many Jews have
excelled, because love of learning and
learning itself are God-directed
obligations designed to help each

person become what he was created to
be: a son of God.

Religious Practices of Judaism

Almost everyone is familiar with the
stories of Adam and Eve, Noah and
the Flood, Samson and the pagan
temple, David and Goliath, Moses and
the parting of the waters of the Red
Sea, and the days of creation. They
are part of the religious folklore of
Western civilization and play a major
role in the religious training of children
raised in the Judeo-Christian tradition.
They have come into the literary and
religious history of the world from the
Hebrew Bible which is the Old
Testament of Christian faith.

But they are more than stories. They
tell profound religious truths. What
they tell is the central belief *about* God
of the Jewish people: that Yahweh is a
saving God.

A young Canadian Jewish boy studies intently in
Hebrew school

Conservative *bas mitzvah*

While the story of the Exodus is the principal story of the Hebrew Bible and the one around which the other stories, the prayers, rituals, and traditions revolve, it is only one of the stories about their God's saving actions in the history of the Jewish people. It is this history that the Jewish people recall and celebrate in their religious practices, festivals, services, and rituals, and it is in these festivals, rituals, and practices that Judaism can best be understood.

Of primary importance to the Jews is respect for the Bible. It is read and studied diligently, and it is also treated with utmost respect. For the Jews, the Bible is the word of God. For them it is The Law. When it is taken from the Ark (a receptacle in the temple or the synagogue reserved for the Bible), people stand. When it is touched, a special piece of paper or other material is used to preserve it from the stains of handling. If a pious Jew wishes to kiss the Bible, he touches his prayer shawl to the page and then raises the fringe of the shawl to his lips. Great care is taken in transcribing the Bible, and many Jewish Bibles, especially those in temples or synagogues, are richly inscribed and decorated. Many Jews take pride in being able to recite long passages from the Bible by heart, particularly from the Pentateuch.

Next in importance is the observance of the Sabbath, about which we have already spoken. Third is the role of the family, and fourth is the importance of the community. Every community, if it is at all possible, has a synagogue, or meeting place for prayer, services, study, and meetings.

---

*"*Bar Mitzvah* means "Son of the Law." Some Reform Congregations have an equivalent or identical ceremony for girls, called a *Bas Mitzvah*. A few Conservative and Orthodox Congregations have a slightly different ceremony for girls.

Hannukah candles outside synagogue

In fifth place is the **Bar Mitzvah** ceremony. This is the ceremony in which young boys in their twelfth or thirteenth year are inducted as adults into the community.* A boy, after long instruction in the Bible and in the Law, is formally inducted into the congregation, and pledges that he will be faithful to the Law, acknowledging that he understands the Law and his responsibility to observe it. The Bar Mitzvah is considered by most Jewish males to be the highlight of their Jewish religious experience.

In sixth place in Jewish religious practices is the observance of the Jewish festivals, or holidays. These are observed in the home and in the temples or synagogues with solemn rituals prescribed for each separate festival. They recall and celebrate the major events in Jewish history and emphasize the saving actions of God in relationship to the Jewish people. Among the more important festivals are:

Rosh Hashana, the Jewish New Year. It is celebrated at the beginning of the seventh month of the Jewish lunar calendar, *Tishri,* which occurs in September or October. It recalls the creation of the world (over 5700 years ago according to Jewish reckoning),** the Day of Judgment, and the need for repentance. It begins the most solemn season of the Jewish year and is the first day of the Ten Days of Repentence or Return, often referred to as the High Holy Days. The Days of Repentence end with Yom Kippur.

Yom Kippur is the Day of Atonement. It is the most solemn day of the Jewish year. It is the day of penitence when Jews ask for forgiveness of sins committed by individuals and by the Jewish people as a nation. Jews believe that sins will not be forgiven unless sorrow and making amends for a particular sin is completed.

Hannukah, or Festival of Lights, is celebrated in December and recalls the

161

victory of the Maccabees over the Syrian army, the recapturing of the city of Jerusalem, and the rededication of the Temple in Jerusalem in 165 B.C.

Sukkot, the festival of Booths or Tabernacles, is celebrated at harvest time in thanksgiving for the benefits of the harvest. It is called "Booths" or "Tabernacles" (dwelling place) because many pious Jews build temporary shelters to recall God's care for the Jews in their desert wanderings during the Exodus when they had only temporary shelters.

Pesach, or Passover, is the celebration of the Jewish deliverance from slavery in Egypt. It is celebrated on the fourteenth day of *Nisan* (in March/April). It is celebrated with the **Seder** meal, at home, during which the story of the deliverance is told and special foods are eaten to recall that the Hebrews ate in haste as they prepared to leave Egypt under the leadership of Moses.

Shavuot, or Festival of Weeks, is celebrated exactly seven weeks after the Passover. It celebrates the proclamation of the Ten Commandments when God gave the Law to the Jewish people.

Tishah B'ab, the ninth day of the month of *Ab* (August) recalls the destruction of the Temple in Jerusalem, the loss of Jewish independence, and other sad events in Jewish history. It is a day of grief for many Jews—they avoid any activities not in keeping with their grief and recite Biblical materials like the Lamentations of Jeremiah, who mourned over the lack of faith of the Jewish people and at the punishments that God was visiting on his unfaithful people.

Purim, celebrated in March, is a joyful festival recalling the victory of the Jews over the Persians. They were saved from extinction by Esther, Jewish wife of Ahaseurus, king of the Persians in the fifth century B.C.

The Structure of Judaism

There is no formal hierarchical or judicial structure in Judaism. There has not been a priesthood since the destruction of the Temple in Jerusalem in 70 A.D., when Jewish sacrifices of animals were discontinued.

Each Jewish congregation is autonomous (a Jew may or may not belong to a congregation) and responsible for its own affairs. It may belong to a confederation, union, or conference, but these are for activities dealing with Jewish affairs, not with the Jewish religion. Each congregation, if possible, has a *rabbi,* or master teacher, whose authority stems from his knowledge, not his position. Rabbis are trained and "ordained" for their position, which is to act as a teacher, guide, and leader of ceremonies accompanying Jewish festivals or life celebrations like birth, the Bar Mitzvah, marriage, and death. He is responsible for the spiritual welfare of the congregation. In Reform and some Conservative congregations there can be women rabbis.

Rabbis in particular geographical areas many times belong to Councils formed of rabbis of particular kinds of Judaism: Orthodox, Conservative, or Reform. These groups function as general policy groups; they have no power over particular congregations or individual Jews.

Perhaps the distinguishing characteristic of Judaism is its

emphasis on conduct, the Jewish character, or spirit, and the ceremonial celebration of life in its religious, cultural, and sociological aspects. For Jews, all of life is religious: each action ought to be done in response to God's will as that will is spelled out in the Torah and the Talmud.

Eastern Orthodox Christians

There are about 4 million Eastern Orthodox Christians in North America of about 123 million worldwide.* They are divided among 15 groups and some 10 independent Churches.

The name *Eastern Orthodox* refers to those Christians who accept the beliefs, religious practices, and organization of the Christian Church established in the major cities of the Eastern Roman Empire during the first three centuries of Christianity. These include the original **Patriarchates** (cities in which the chief bishop resides) of Constantinople (modern Istanbul) in Turkey, Alexandria in Egypt, Antioch in Syria, and Jerusalem. These were founded, Eastern Orthodox Christians assert, by the apostles of Jesus. Late Patriarchates were founded in other cities of the Empire, and all together formed the Catholic Church. When the Churches of the East and the West split over important doctrinal statements, those who joined with the

---

*It is difficult to tell how many Eastern Orthodox Christians there are worldwide because no one knows how many there are in Russia, originally one of the largest branches in the Eastern Orthodox community of Churches.

Eastern bloc became the Eastern Orthodox Churches.

Eastern Orthodox Churches include those in Russia, Greece, Armenia, Albania, Yugoslavia, Bulgaria, Cyprus, Rumania, the Republic of Georgia, and independent branches established in other countries of the Middle East and Eastern Europe. All the principal groups have "missions" or congregations in Poland, Finland, Japan, Uganda, Tanzania, and the Americas. The greatest number of Eastern Orthodox Christians in North America live in the United States; they belong to two major branches, the Greek Orthodox Church and the Russian Orthodox Church.

For centuries the Eastern Orthodox Churches called themselves the "Greek Orthodox Church" because early Christianity was identified in its language and customs as Greek, and because, when the split between the Eastern and the Western (Rome-centered) Churches occurred, the Eastern Churches considered themselves "orthodox," that is, correct in theological opinion and religious doctrine and practice. Later, the word *Greek* was dropped from the national Church name, and the various Church groups became known by their national name. Thus, the Russian Orthodox Greek Church became the Russian Orthodox Church. Now, the various Orthodox Churches are known as the Eastern Orthodox Churches.

What Is an Eastern Orthodox Christian?

As we said above, an Eastern Orthodox Christian is one who accepts the doctrinal positions of the Orthodox Churches, uses the ancient liturgies of

Kalenic Monastery, Serbia (c. 1425)

St. Michael's Cathedral,
Sitka, Alaska

the Eastern Churches in his worship, and observes the religious practices of the Christian Church in vogue in the eleventh century.

For the first ten centuries of the Christian era, Christianity was "one, holy, catholic, and apostolic." That is, it was "one" in doctrine and practice; "holy" in its founder and in its "means of grace"; "catholic" because it was meant for all people everywhere; and "apostolic" in its origin—founded by the apostles of Jesus.

There was, of course, diversity in various local Churches in language and culture, but there was unity in doctrine and in practice.

For the first several years, the center of the Church was in the east. As the Church spread, the Western Church, centered in Rome, became more and more powerful, and because St. Peter had been the bishop of Rome, the Roman bishop was considered the titular head of the Church. In the seventh and eighth centuries, uneasiness spread in the Eastern half of the Church over the power of the "Patriarch of Rome," the Pope. More and more he was being challenged by the Patriarchs of the East, but no serious threat to unity was mounted. Then, in 1054, due as much to social, political, cultural, and military causes as to doctrinal ones, the Christian Church split into two separate divisions: the Eastern Church and the Western Church. Since that time, they have gone their separate ways. Attempts at reunion have been made from time to time but, though the atmosphere is cordial in discussions, no real progress has been made.

For centuries, Eastern Orthodox Christianity confined itself to the Eastern part of the old Roman Empire, with the exception of the mission groups sent by the Russian Orthodox Church to the Far East, including many missions to Russian Siberia.

Eastern Orthodox Christianity came to North America relatively late in the development of the New World when compared to other Christian groups. It was not until the nineteenth and early twentieth centuries that Eastern Orthodox Christians came in large numbers to the New World because of political upheavals in Eastern Europe. They came from Bulgaria, Serbia, Greece, Russia, Syria, Lebanon, Egypt, and the Ukraine to settle mostly in the United States. Independent Patriarchates were established in some few cases, but, for the most part, Eastern Orthodox Christians have their ecclesiastical, liturgical, doctrinal, governmental, and cultural roots in Eastern Orthodox Christianity.

What Do Eastern Orthodox Christians Believe?

Eastern Orthodox Christians, unlike most Protestant groups, accept all the beliefs, doctrinal statements and explanations of those statements as they were held by the entire Christian Church for 1,000 years. It was not until the separation of 1054, precipitated by a dispute in the explanation of the nature of the relationship of the Three Persons of the Trinity, that the Eastern Orthodox Churches and the Western Church began to go their separate ways. (This was only the tip of the iceberg. What really caused the separation was the political power-play being played out more or less behind the scenes between the Eastern half of the old Roman Empire and the Western half.)

There were, of course, other things that separated the Eastern Church from the Western Church, but they were all relatively minor and mostly cultural and jurisdictional, such as married clergy in the East, the Pope's intervening in political affairs of the East, the date of the celebration of Easter, the true nature of the Pope's authority in the Church, and the like. In spite of these differences, however, there was unity in faith, doctrine, and the sacraments.

When the split occurred, the Eastern Churches denied that the Pope had supreme and final authority in any matters pertaining to the Church and refused to accept any of his decisions in matters of faith, morals, worship, or religious practice. They did not say that he was wrong; they just refused to recognize that he had jurisdiction over them. From that point on, the Pope was not even consulted; it was as if the Western Church did not exist. As far as the Eastern Churches were concerned, it was the Western Church that had separated from the Church. As time went on, the rift between the Eastern Church and the Western Church widened despite attempts from time to time to heal the breach and bring the two parts of the Christian Church together.

The degree of misunderstanding grew greater, and the Easterners' conception of themselves as Orthodox took on a new sense. They were Orthodox in that they had resisted not only the ancient Christological heresies but also the Latins' dangerous innovations; they now represented the immutable faith of the past. For many years, the term "Orthodox" was unknown in the West and no one was sure

how to describe this separate Christian entity. "The Greeks" . . . was incorrect since the majority of adherents to the Eastern Church were Russians. "A Greco-Slav" Church was incorrect also, since it con-

tained Arabs, Syrians, Rumanians, and Georgians. . . . It was not until the twentieth century that the custom became established of referring to them as Orthodox Churches, partly for the sake of simplicity and partly in recognition of an established fact. . . .

—Henri Daniel-Rops, *Our Brothers in Christ* (New York: E.P. Dutton Company, 1967), page 263.

Triptych (Greek, Post-Byzantine, c. 1600 AD). Elvehjem Art Center, University of Wisconsin, Madison. Gift of Joseph E. Davies.

In spite of the fact that from the eleventh century on the Eastern Church refused to accept any doctrinal, liturgical, or jurisdictional decrees of the Popes of the Western Church, the doctrinal bases for Christianity in both parts of the Christian Church remained intact. Like the Western Church, members of the Eastern Orthodox Churches believe in the doctrine of the Trinity, in the divinity of Christ, the virginity of Mary, the incarnation, the role of the Church in people's salvation, immortality, the need for salvation-in-Christ, the nature of the sacraments, the necessity of apostolic succession, and so forth.

The beliefs of the Eastern Churches are summed up in the traditional Christian creeds: the **Apostles' Creed** and the Nicene Creed. They believe in the oneness of God and in the Trinity of Persons in God. They believe that God is the Creator of all things, that the Son is the redeemer of people, and that the Holy Spirit is the Sanctifier. They believe that the Son of God (Jesus) became a human being and that his birth, life, death and resurrection affected the salvation of all people.

They believe that the Church is the body of Christ through which the Holy Spirit sanctifies people and through which the people worship God. They believe in the sacramental nature of the traditional seven sacraments, in the resurrection of the dead, and in eternal life with God after death. From these come all the other credal aspects of the Eastern Orthodox Churches, interpreted to give meaning to them in light of how the Eastern Orthodox Christians understand them.

Religious Practices of Eastern Orthodox Christians

To those only passingly familiar with Eastern Orthodoxy, it is identified with ornate Churches, a right-to-left sign of the cross, a bearded hierarchy, ancient and mystifying liturgies, richly ornamented, brocade vestments, and "eastern" customs. For Eastern Orthodox Christians, however, these are only signs and symbols of a rich tradition based on a philosophy of religion which puts greater emphasis on the proper worship of God than it does on social relevance. The religious practices of Eastern Orthodox Christians are based on a tradition that goes back to the philosophy and practice of the "Greek Fathers"—the Church leaders of early Christian days who not only gave deep philosophical meaning to the Incarnation but also established the philosophy of religious practice which still governs Eastern Orthodox practices.

The principal religious action of Eastern Orthodox Christians is what they call the "Divine Liturgy." It is similar to the Roman Catholic Mass and is somewhat analogous to the

Priest saying Easter Mass behind *iconostas,* St. Mary's Orthodox Church, Chelsea, Massachusetts

Protestant Communion services. It is the official, public liturgical act of the Eastern Orthodox Churches. It is a solemn, stylized, "eastern ritualized" worship service designed to honor and worship God in a style and manner befitting his divine majesty.

For the service of the Divine Liturgy, Orthodox Churches are built in the form of a cross whose arms project equally from the center of the Church over which a dome is built. The eastern arm of the cross is divided from the rest of the Church by a large, richly ornamented screen, called an **iconostas,** behind which the "holy **mysteries**" are enacted on an altar reserved for this purpose.

The holy mysteries, or the Sacrament of the Eucharist, or the Eucharistic Service, commonly called "Holy Communion," is, for Eastern Orthodox Christians, a divine drama re-enacting the life of Christ. The ceremonies of the Sacrament of the Eucharist are based on the pattern of worship established by the Greek Fathers, principally John Chrysostom, after whom the most used liturgy is named.

Although the Divine Liturgy is one action in itself, it can be divided into three major parts. Part one is the preparation, called the "Morning Service," during which the materials of the Sacrifice are prepared. It recalls the incarnation and birth of Christ.

Part two consists of the "Processions." The first is the entrance procession when the litany is said, prayers are offered, and the sermon is given. This is followed by the "Gospel procession" when the Bible is brought out, an epistle is read, and the Gospel is chanted or read by the priest. This symbolizes Jesus coming to the people

169

to teach them and to heal their ills. The third procession is the "Great Entrance" when the prepared gifts are brought out—the bread and the wine—and appropriate prayers are said. The Creed is then recited, and hymns and prayers of praise to God as Almighty are offered.

Part three is the Communion Service. After the Great Entrance ceremony is completed, the priest goes to the altar behind the screen, and the Consecration Service of the bread and the wine takes place. When this is completed, the priest carries the chalice, into which the consecrated bread has been placed, in procession to the people and distributes Holy Communion to all who wish to partake. This symbolizes Christ giving himself to his people for their salvation. The Divine Liturgy ends with the Dismissal Service which includes a prayer of thanksgiving to God for his goodness in giving the Divine Mysteries to his people and a blessing of the people by the priest.

The Eucharistic, or Communion, Service is the highlight of Eastern Orthodox Divine Liturgy. Eastern Orthodox Christians believe that the bread and wine are changed into the body and blood of Christ and that each person who receives Holy Communion receives the body and blood of Christ. They believe that this is the highlight of Christ's mission on earth—when he came to give himself completely, though in a mysterious way, to his people. Their entire Divine Liturgy is built around this fact for them; it is done in response to the command of Christ to "do this in memory of me" when he said, "Take and eat, this is my body."

The principal language of the Divine liturgy is Greek—the Greek used when the Greek Fathers patterned the Liturgy. At the present time, native languages may be used for some of the service, especially that part which is directed to the people. The Divine Liturgy is long, lasting up to three hours in most cases. The people, however, need not be present for the entire service—they often come only for the Communion Service or for the Great Entrance.

The Eucharist is the principal sacrament of Eastern Orthodoxy. The other six sacraments, or "Holy Mysteries," as they are called, are the traditional sacraments of united Christianity. Baptism is conferred by triple immersion, and Confirmation is administered immediately after Baptism no matter what the age of the baptized. Confession is made to a priest, and the sick and the dying are anointed. Only men are ordained priests in Eastern Orthodox Churches, and only unmarried priests can be consecrated bishops. People are married in an elaborate liturgical service which by its nature is sacramental. All the sacraments are sacred actions for **Orthodox Christians**, who believe that God is acting in them through his Church. They are an important and integral part of the religious life of all Orthodox Christians.

Orthodox Christians venerate the saints, especially the Virgin Mary, have a strong devotional life of prayer and sacrifice, and promote vocations to the monastic life. There are religious orders of men and women in Eastern Orthodoxy where the traditions of dedicating oneself "to religion" date back to the first centuries of Christianity.

One more religious practice peculiar to Eastern Orthodox Churches is the

date of their celebration of the major Christian feasts. Eastern Orthodox Churches follow the Julian calendar, rather than the Gregorian calendar in use in most countries of the world.* Eastern Orthodox Christians celebrate Christmas and New Year's Day thirteen days after other Christian Churches—on January 7 and 14.

Easter in Orthodox Churches is celebrated on the first Sunday following the full moon after the coming of spring, but always after the Hebrew Passover. Western Christians celebrate Easter on the first Sunday after the first full moon after the coming of spring, regardless of the date of the Jewish Passover.

*The Julian calendar was started by Julius Caesar in 46 B.C. It had 365 days except every four years when it had 366. Pope Gregory XIII updated the calendar in 1582 and made minor adjustments to allow for inaccuracies that creep into any calendar.

Occasionally, Easter may coincide in Eastern and Western Christianity, as in 1980, but it might be as many as thirty-five days later, as it was in 1975.

The Organization of the Eastern Orthodox Church

Eastern Orthodox Churches are organized along hierarchical lines. Men are ordained as deacons, priests, or bishops to fulfill a sacred ministry and to govern the Church. After extensive training, men are ordained deacons and then priests to serve in the sacred ministry of a parish. Bishops are elected from among the priests by a synod of bishops to administer a diocese, or area, and assume their office upon enthronement in a particular diocese or Church.

Each independent Orthodox Church within the Eastern Orthodox group of Churches is divided into dioceses whose head may be a "metropolitan," that is the head of a particular Church district; an "archbishop," that is, the head of a group of Churches within a district or several districts; or a "Patriarch," the head of one of the original metropolitan sees (Constantinople, Jerusalem, Antioch, and Alexandria) or one of the principal cities in major countries of the world. Patriarchates can only be established by the consent of all the Patriarchs, who hold the highest office in the Eastern Orthodox Churches.

No one person is head of the Eastern Orthodox Churches. Each Church is independently administered by a synod of bishops, called a Council. The Patriarch of Constantinople, the oldest Patriarchical see, is considered the spiritual leader of world Orthodoxy and is referred to as "the first among equals." He is often called the "Ecumenical Patriarch" to signify his place of dignity among the other Patriarchs with whom he shares leadership in the Eastern Orthodox Churches.

Even though the Eastern Orthodox Churches have maintained a low profile in the religious life of North America, there is no doubt about the importance of Eastern Orthodox beliefs and practices in the religious life of the members of the various Orthodox groups. Eastern Orthodoxy brings a sense of tradition, dignity, and solemnity to the worship of God in North America and is a reminder of the heritage from which all Christianity sprang.

The Mormons

The term *Mormon* is commonly used to identify a member of the Church of Jesus Christ of Latter-day Saints. The title *Mormon* comes from a man named Mormon, a prophet of the Church who, Mormons believe, lived in North America during "the thousand years" (600 B.C. to 421 A.D.). Mormons believe that this prophet kept a record of the prophets and people who lived in North America (and were the ancestors of the American Indians) as a remnant of the "House of Israel" who left Jerusalem and eventually found their way to North America. His records, and other materials, are contained in *The Book of Mormon*, one of the scriptures of the Church of Jesus Christ of Latter-day Saints. It is because of their identification with *The Book of Mormon* that members of the Church of Jesus Christ of the Latter-day Saints are called "Mormons."

The proper title of the Church of Jesus Christ of Latter-day Saints identifies what the Church is. It is a Church that accepts Jesus Christ as the Son of God who came to save people from their sins. For Mormons, their Church is the Church of Jesus Christ. It is called "of Latter-day Saints" to distinguish it from the Church of "former" (that is, earlier) days which, Mormons contend, fell away from the Church of Jesus Christ shortly after the first century A.D.* Mormons believe that the Church of Jesus Christ was restored in 1820 when God appeared to Joseph Smith near Palmyra, New York, and ordered him to restore the Church as it was in ancient days.

> I saw two Personages, whose brightness and glory defy all description, standing above me in the air. One of them spake unto me, calling me by name, and said, pointing to the other: "This is my Beloved Son. Hear Him!"
> —Pearl of Great Price 2:17

There are about four million Mormons, worldwide, divided into two major groups, and five or six smaller groups. The largest, and best known, is the Church of Jesus Christ of Latter-day Saints headquartered in Salt Lake City, Utah.** This group has about

3,250,000 members, 80% of whom live in the United States. There are about 70,000 members worshipping in 290 Churches in Canada.

The second largest group, headquartered in Independence, Missouri, is the Re-organized Church of Jesus Christ of Latter-day Saints, with over 200,000 members. Other Mormon groups with much smaller memberships are located mostly in midwestern United States. The Mormons have sent missionaries to Mexico and have had some success there.

What Is a Mormon?

As mentioned above, a Mormon is a member of the Church of Jesus Christ of Latter-day Saints founded in the first half of the nineteenth century by Joseph Smith. Although it is a "Church of Jesus Christ" and its members believe many of the things that Roman Catholic, Eastern Orthodox, and Protestant Christians believe, it is neither Roman Catholic, Orthodox, nor Protestant. It is a new Church whose beliefs, religious practices, and structure are based on the revelations to Joseph Smith, on the Christian Bible as explained by Joseph Smith and the elders of the Mormon Church, on *The Book of Mormon,* an ancient scripture Joseph Smith said was given to him and which he translated, on the *Pearl of Great Price,* a book containing Joseph Smith's testimony of his visions and the revelations he received in the visions, and on the *Doctrines and Covenants,* a collection of the reported revelations of Joseph Smith and others.

Mormonism arose during the third decade of the nineteenth century in western New York State. It was a period of intense religious agitation,

---

Saints, or "holy ones", is a word that many New Testament writers use to signify the members of the Church of Jesus. It is so used by the Mormons.

**Approximately half the people in Utah are Mormons. The Church runs the largest Church-related University in the United States: Brigham Young University with more than 30,000 students.

known in history as the Great Awakening, when ministers of various sects put forth great effort to gain converts to their particular persuasion.*

*See pages 92-3.

Joseph Smith (1805-1844), a bright, religiously inclined boy was affected by all the religious turmoil. Recalling those days in later years, he wrote:

> . . . the whole district of country seemed affected by it, and great

Joseph Smith preaching to Indians

Sunstone from the facade of the destroyed Nauvoo, Illinois Temple built by Joseph Smith

multitudes united themselves to the different parties, which created no small stir and division amongst the people . . . so great were the confusion and strife among the different denominations, that it was impossible for a person as young as I was, and so unacquainted with men and things, to come to any certain conclusion who was right and who was wrong. In the midst of this war of words and tumult of opinions, I often said to myself, What is to be done? Who of all these parties are right; or, are they all wrong together? If any one of them be right, which is it, and how shall I know it? While laboring under the extreme difficulties caused by the contests of these parties of religionists, I was one day reading the Epistle of James, first chapter and *fifth verse, which reads:* If any of you lack wisdom, let him ask of God, that giveth to all men liberally, and upbraideth not; and it shall be given him. *Never did any passage of scripture come with more power to the heart of man than this did at this time to mine. It seemed to enter with great force into every feeling of my heart. I reflected on it again and again, knowing that if any person needed wisdom from God, I did; for how to act I did not know, and unless I could get more wisdom than I had, I would never know.*

—Extracts from the *History of Joseph Smith* verses 2-12. (Salt Lake City, Utah: Deseret Book Company, *n.d.*).

Shortly thereafter (1820), Smith had what he said was his first revelation when God the Father and Jesus appeared to him. From that time on he worked tirelessly to find out what God's will for him was.

On September 21, 1823, when he was eighteen years old, Smith tells us that a heavenly messenger named Moroni appeared several times to him and told him that he was chosen for a special work by God. In 1827, Moroni again appeared to him and gave him the gold plates on which the prophet Mormon, the father of Moroni, had written the record of ancient America which told of the early faith of the Indians and of their falling away from that faith. Moroni, according to Smith, told him that he had buried the plates fourteen hundred years before (when he was still a man) in a stone box at Cumorah, a hill in western New York State.

Joseph Smith said that he was ordered by Moroni to translate the materials written by Mormon in ancient Egyptian. He did so, he said, with a special set of translating instruments provided by Moroni. He finished his translation in 1830 and published it as *The Book of Mormon.* It is the most sacred book of the Mormons and is the basis for the structure and purpose of the Church of Jesus Christ of Latter-day Saints.

The Book of Mormon, containing fifteen "books"** in the manner of the Bible, contains, Mormons believe, the record of the original inhabitants of North America, the Indians, who were descendants of one of the tribes of Israel that left Jerusalem after the Babylonian Captivity of the Jews (537 B.C.) It tells how two sons fell away from the true faith, and their descendants were cursed with dark skin. An important implication in the book is that Jesus came to North America (the "land of promise" according to Smith) after his resurrection and promised that the Church would be brought there to the lost tribes of the House of Israel (3 Nephi 17:4 and 11:8-10).

After completing his preparation of *The Book of Mormon,* Smith organized his Church with twenty-two followers. He had great success among the people but encountered difficulties with the established religions and with civil authorities because of his "revelations" and his "strange doctrines" (such as defending the Indians, and practicing polygamy). He moved his group to Kirtland, Ohio, then to a location in Missouri, near Independence, which he called "Zion" because, he said, the Garden of Eden had been located

---

**Totalling 300,000 words.

Joseph Smith's Mansion House, Nauvoo, Illinois

Nauvoo, Illinois circa 1840

Old Carthage Jail, Carthage, Illinois

Kirtland, Ohio, Temple

Joseph Smith homestead, Nauvoo, Illinois

Joseph Smith being murdered

In restoring the Church of Jesus Christ, Smith ordered several things he said had been abandoned by the apostate Churches (the Roman Catholics and the Protestants). He not only re-established tithing (the giving of ten percent of one's worldly goods to the Church), but he also established the office of apostles, prophets, pastors, the Aaronite priesthood, teachers, evangelists, the office of high-priest, the "seventies," elders, bishops, deacons, and the Council of Twelve (who govern the Church). All these he restored between 1829 and 1840. They all remain integral parts of the structure of the Mormon Church.

Brigham Young (1801–1877)

there. The group was finally evicted from Missouri and settled in Nauvoo, Illinois, about two hundred fifty miles southwest of Chicago. There they built a city of some twenty thousand people, the largest in Illinois at the time, and prospered until trouble broke out again.

Just what caused the trouble has been debated for years. Whatever it was, Joseph Smith and the leaders of the Mormons were jailed in Carthage, Illinois, just a few miles away, and Smith was murdered by a mob dressed as Indians. Shortly thereafter, some of Smith's followers, under the leadership of Brigham Young, left for Utah; others, notably Smith's widow and sons, remained in Nauvoo and formed the Reorganized Church of Jesus Christ of Latter-day Saints, disputing Brigham Young's claim of leadership of the Church.

Young Mormon missionaries visiting prospective converts

Joseph Smith had received the restored priesthood, or authority to act for God, as was promised earlier. This he received from the Apostles Peter, James and John under the direction of Jesus Christ. The Church of Jesus Christ of Latter-day Saints was established with the same organization that existed in the Primitive Church during Christ's earthly ministry, with Apostles, Prophets and other callings so mentioned in the Holy Bible. Through his appointed Prophets God has revealed and will further yet reveal many great and important things to the world.

—Chris Kirsch, *The Church of Jesus Christ of the Latter-day Saints*, (unpublished ms.), page 4.

The Mormon Church today is one of the most highly organized religious bodies in North America and one of the most affluent. It is highly evangelistic, as all who are able to are required to spend part of their youth in missionary work. There are over 26,000 missionaries, most of whom are young men about nineteen years of age who spend two years of their life to staff missions in all parts of the world. The Mormon Church is growing at a rate of about eight percent per year in the United States and has grown by twenty percent in Canada in the last ten years.

What Mormons Believe

The Mormon belief system and the doctrinal explanations of their beliefs are based on the conviction that God continually revealed himself and his will to Joseph Smith in direct, visual revelations from himself, Jesus, angels, prophets, and Jesus' apostles.* Because of these revelations, Mormons depart radically from Protestant and Roman Catholic views about God, the nature and destiny of people, and religious practice even though all three use the Christian Bible as their primary source for knowing about God and people's relationship with God. Among the more important Mormon beliefs are the following:

The Eternity of Matter. Perhaps the keystone Mormon belief and the one that for them makes sense of all their other beliefs, is that the "elements"—matter, intelligence, and energy—are eternal; that is, they always existed. In other words, Mormons do not believe that God created the world; he simply "organized" it. For Mormons, "spirit" is simply matter that cannot be seen except by "purer" eyes and cannot be felt except by "purer" beings. This

*For example, Smith said he had seven direct revelations in Nauvoo and two direct revelations in Ramus, Illinois, between January 19, 1841 and July 12, 1843 concerning the nature of matter and creation.

Temple, Salt Lake City, Utah

belief in the eternity of matter and its dynamic activity enables Mormons to believe certain things about God and about people's relationship to God and their destiny that are totally different from traditional Christian beliefs even though certain things in both are somewhat similar (in language, if not in meaning).

The Nature of God. For Mormons, God is a material being, who once was a man on earth and is now an exalted and perfect man of flesh and bones (he attained this status by working to become perfect), residing near the planet "Kolob".

> God himself was once as we are now, and is an exalted man, and sits enthroned in yonder heavens! . . . if the veil were rent today . . . you would see him like a man in form. . . .
>
> We have imagined and supposed that God was God from all eternity. I will refute that idea. . . . It is the first principle of the Gospel . . . that he was once a man like us . . . and you have got to be Gods yourselves, and to be kings and priests to God, the same as all Gods have done before you, namely by going from one small degree to another. . . .
>
> —Joseph Smith, "Lectures on Faith," quoted in *The Mormons*, Thomas F. O'Dea. (Chicago: Phoenix Books / The University of Chicago Press, 1957, page 55).

Jesus was created by God and won out in a battle with Lucifer (the chief angel) over doing God's will. He came to earth and now lives as a man with flesh and bones in "the heavens." The Holy Spirit is a "spirit body" not having flesh and bones and "activates" people on earth. Thus, for the Mormons, God is Trinity, but is a Trinity of three distinct, literal personages, all of whom arose in a particular time.

The Nature of People. Mormons believe that God procreated (through sexual intercourse with a female god) an untold number of souls who are waiting in heaven for bodies to be made on earth so that they can make the transition to godhood through the experience of human life.

The most important thing a Mormon can do on earth is to improve himself as a human being (this is the reason for the strict moral code of Mormonism) and to develop those qualities which will enable him to attain the highest degree of exaltation in the heavenly life. Obviously, therefore, Mormons believe in the resurrection of the human body.

Salvation. Mormons believe that everyone will be "saved" but not all to the same degree. (There are, according to Mormon beliefs, some "Sons of Perdition" who will not be saved, but their fate is not known.) Some of the saved will experience a kind of limited life on earth; some will enter exaltation in the "degrees of glory" earned by obedience to the universal law of the Mormon Church.

This salvation takes place in two phases. The first is after death and before resurrection, but when this will occur is not known for each individual. The second is after the resurrection, when those saved will enjoy one of three degrees of exaltation. The highest degree is the one in which a person enjoys God's presence.

The highest degree can only be attained by those who have observed all the laws, ordinances, and commandments faithfully and who have been married in a temple ceremony which seals a man and a woman as husband and wife for all eternity—they shall live in the next life as husband and wife also. If they have followed all the prescriptions faithfully, they may achieve full godhood and be put in charge of one of the planets to rule as the planet's god. Mormons who marry "outsiders" cannot achieve this "celestial" glory.

Mormons also believe that the time of final salvation—the **Millenium**—is near at hand. They believe that Jesus will appear "in glory in the clouds of heaven" in Zion (near Independence, Missouri) where a great Temple is being readied, and in Jerusalem.*

Revelation. Mormons believe that God reveals himself and his will to people. They believe that he spoke to Adam and to the early Patriarchs who recorded their revelations which have since been lost. They believe he spoke directly to the **Prophets**—both of Israel and to those who emigrated to North America. They believe that his revelations are recorded in the Christian Bible (but mistranslated in some cases by later scribes), and in *The Book of Mormon,* in the *Pearl of Great Price,* and in the *Doctrines and Covenants,* both of which reveal not only the revelations of Joseph Smith, but of other leading Mormons as well. They also believe in the immediacy of revelation; that is, that their own living prophets, apostles, Council of Twelve, and their President speak for God by making revelations from time to time

Spencer Kimball, world leader of the Church of Jesus Christ of Latter-day Saints

Joseph Freeman, first black Mormon priest, with family

*In 1978, the Mormons completed a land deal with the Israelis enabling them to build a Temple in Jerusalem for the re-appearance of Jesus.

about Mormon doctrine and practice. They believe, for example, that God spoke to Wilford Woodruff, Church President in 1890, and did away with polygamy, and that he spoke to Spencer Kimball and the Council of Twelve in 1978 and told them to allow blacks to be ordained priests.

Mormons hold the Bible to be Word of God, insofar as it is correctly translated. They believe that God "organized" (but did not create) the world in six days, that the forbidden fruit of the Garden of Eden was sexual temptation, that Adam and Eve were driven from the Garden of Eden (in Missouri) by an angel, that there was a flood as described in Genesis, that Samson destroyed the pagan temple by brute force, that Jonah lived in the belly of some great fish, and so forth. They do not recognize the scholarship of Biblical authorities outside of the Mormon Church.

The Restored Church. Mormons believe that Joseph Smith received a new revelation about the Church. They believe that the religion of both "Apostate Jews" and "of the papal, Greek, and Protestant Churches" of the nineteenth centuries to be false because they changed the nature and structure of the Church as God and Jesus had founded it. To restore the Church, Joseph Smith and his early leaders formed "the true Church of Jesus Christ" with all the structures, orders, ministries, and practices of the Church that Jesus organized in the first century. They wanted no part of "the great Apostasy of the Christian Churches."*

But the restoration, "after seventeen centuries of falsehoods," was not simply to be a restoration of orders, ministries, and practices Joseph Smith and his early followers thought were part of the Christian Church of the first century. It was a restoration of purpose. Joseph Smith's Church was to be a restoration of the "New Israel." It was to be a gathering of the people of God to bring a new order, a new Kingdom of God on earth. The people were to work hard, both religiously and in their secular work, to make this kingdom a reality. The new Church was to be a city of God, bringing all who believed and obeyed into a "New Jerusalem" fit to greet Christ in his "Second Coming." This could only be achieved by "faith in the Lord Jesus" and accepting the rule of the Church in every aspect of one's life. Life was to be lived for the Church and the realization of its purposes and goals.

For the true Mormon, the Church of Jesus Christ of Latter-day Saints was a divinely predicted and divinely implemented act of God inaugurated by Joseph Smith, God's prophet in the sense of the Old Testament and apostle in the sense of the New Testament. For Mormons, the Church of Jesus Christ of Latter-day Saints is the only true Church.**

Mormons, of course, have many other beliefs and doctrines, but they are all spin-offs of these principal concepts. It is from these, too, that Mormon religious practices stem. Some of them are widely known, like their missionary work and their abstaining from alcohol, tobacco, and coffee. Others are less known, and some few are known only to Mormons.

*Orson Pratt, a series of pamphlets on "The Doctrines of the Gospel," quoted by Thomas O'Dea in *The Mormons,* p. 134.

**James E. Talmadge, *Articles of Faith,* (Salt Lake City, Utah: Church of Jesus Christ of Latter-day Saints, 1939), p. 403.

Religious Practices of the Mormons

Every action of a Mormon's life is considered a religious practice, because it is to be done to enable him to gain greater exaltation in the next life. Many Mormons speak of their Church as a way of life. There are, however, many religious practices which are Church actions done specifically as religious practices of the Church. These are conducted in Churches or temples.

The first and most important Mormon religious practice is baptism, by immersion only. For Mormons it is a witness to entering into a covenant with God and of membership in the Church. Infants are not baptized in the Mormon Church because they are too young; the usual age is eight [before that, a baptism is not valid]. Immediately after baptism, a simple "confirmation" ceremony is held by laying on of hands to secure gifts of the Holy Ghost.

A unique aspect of Mormon belief about baptism is what they call **"Baptism for the Dead."** This is a ceremony in which a Mormon is baptized again as a substitute for someone of his relatives, or ancestors, who was not baptized in the Morman Church so that in the afterlife this person may progress toward exaltation before the Millenium.

The Lord's Supper is a simple ceremony. Bread and water (Mormons do not drink wine) are blessed and partaken of by all present for the ceremony.

Sunday worship service is pretty much an all day affair. The men (priests) arrive very early to prepare for the service, and the families arrive later in the morning.

Font for baptism of the dead, Salt Lake City Temple

The service itself is held in a kind of chapel in which the pulpit, or speaker's area, is central. Prayers are said and hymns are sung (Mormons put much emphasis on group singing of hymns). After scripture readings, a sermon is given by a layman especially selected for the job. After the sermon and more hymn singing, the Lord's Supper takes place. The bread and the water are blessed by one of the men of the highest order of Aaronite priesthood and distributed to the seated congregation by some of the members of the lowest order of priesthood. More hymns and prayers are said, then the congregation disperses for further Sunday activities.

Because Mormonism is a family-oriented religion, various members of the family gather for reading, study, prayer, or recreation within the Church area. Late in the day, the family returns home to observe further the

festivals, dances, athletic contests, choirs (the Mormon Tabernacle Choir of Salt Lake City is only one of many famous Mormon choirs), concerts, group travel, junkets to "holy places," and the like, all as part of their religious life.

The Structure of the Mormon Church

A local congregation of Mormons is called a "ward." It usually consists of five to five hundred members, and is presided over by a bishop and two counselors. A number of wards joined together form a "stake," which is presided over by a president, who often is a bishop taken from the ranks of the high priests, and by two counselors who are high priests also. All the stakes are governed by the General Authorities—thirty-four men, the highest of whom holds the First Presidency. The First President is called the "Prophet, Seer, and Revelator." He is assisted by the Council of Twelve, who have eight assistants. Under these are the Council of the Seventies, the Presiding Bishop, and the Patriarch. Members of the General Authorities are appointed for life and are charged with overseeing the spiritual and temporal welfare of the Church.

There is no doubt that the Church of Jesus Christ of Latter-day Saints provides religious security for its members. It is a dynamically active Church: it involves its members in a total religious program and reaches out to convert others to its way. It is a concerned Church: it provides economic, social, and spiritual programs that fulfill its members' deepest religious needs. It is an American Church: it grew out of the

Lord's Day in some appropriate, quiet, religious manner.

The Mormon priesthood is open to any male over twelve years of age in good standing in the community. A Mormon priest might be a teacher, priest, elder, a member of the seventy, a high priest, or bishop. The priest helps administer the affairs of the congregation, baptizes, blesses the Sacrament, and receives the **tithe** offerings. He helps with the teaching and conducts family services in the home. He is admitted to the inner circles of temple worship and usually participates in the **"celestial marriage"** service. Mormon Temples are sacred places of outstanding architecture and beauty and are closed to all but the "worthy."

Mormons emphasize community religious services. Besides the ordinary worship services, the Mormons sponsor parties, dinners, outings, receptions, art

dynamics of nineteenth century American religious realities, and embodies in its teachings and practices the American ideal. For those who belong to it, the Mormon Church is a caring Church that is the center of their lives.

Other Religious Groups Exerting Influence on the Religious and Social Life of North America

There are many people for whom the major religious groups discussed so far provide no secure answer to their religious needs. These people belong to many different Church groups or independent Churches. They are found in every corner of North America. Most of them exert little influence on the religious, cultural, or political life of Canada, the United States, or Mexico.

There are other groups, however, though they are relatively small in numbers when compared to the larger groups, that do have an impact on life in North America. Among those that do have such an impact are:

Jehovah's Witnesses. Most Protestant groups do not recognize the Jehovah Witnesses as Protestant, but the Witnesses of Jehovah consider themselves to be the only possessors of true faith in Christ. They resemble the Seventh-Day Adventists and get their name from the Bible: "You are my witnesses, saith Jehovah, and I am

God." (Isaiah 43: 12) They are unalterably opposed to the concept of the Trinity (though they do believe that Jesus is God), believe that Satan has opposed God from eternity and actively on earth since the Garden of Eden, and that God constantly puts people to the test to avoid sin. They further believe that Jesus opposed Satan and finally overcame him in 1914 when he took power in heaven. Since then, Satan's power has been unleashed on earth and the Witnesses must do everything in their power to convince people to avoid sin; hence their intensive, door-to-door solicitation. They believe that God will punish the wicked with terrible pains in hell, that he will reward the "elect" (the 144,000 mentioned in Revelation 7:4) with power in heaven, and that the remainder will enjoy perfect happiness on earth at the end of time. They are literal in their reading of the Bible, are absolutely opposed to serving in the military and saluting the flag, and forbid blood transfusions. Jehovah Witnesses are militantly evangelical, and every Witness must participate actively in converting people to their faith. They have God for their supreme ruler, but are governed by a committee of ten ordained Witness ministers.

Christian Scientist. Although Christian Scientists are not considered "Protestant" by most traditional Protestants, Christian Scientists call themselves Protestant. Christian Science was founded by Mary Baker Eddy (1821–1910) as "The Church of Christ, Scientist." Its principal belief is that sickness is an imperfection in a person and is cured by spiritual rather than physical means. Christian Scientists believe that any illness, injury, or evil in a person can be

completely cured through prayer. The two principal works upon which Christian Scientism is based are the Gospels (emphasizing the healing mission of Christ) and *Science and Health with Key to the Scriptures*, by Mrs. Eddy.

Seventh-Day Adventist. Seventh-Day Adventists are fundamentalists who observe Saturday, rather than Sunday, as the Sabbath, or Lord's Day. They accept the Bible literally, believing among other things that the world was created in six days exactly as the Bible depicts it and that Christ will come in glory (hence, "Adventist") exactly as it is told in Revelation 6. They believe in the "millenium" (Christ will come and reign on earth for one thousand years), the glory of the "righteous" and the punishment of the "wicked" by fire. They believe in "the signs of the times" that is, that Christ's coming will be preceded by terrible events on earth. Adventists have a strict moral code which includes an absolute injunction against drinking alcohol in any form, smoking, gambling, the use of drugs, and dancing. Adventists are heavily engaged in charitable work and are well known for their hospitals.

Quakers. *Quakers* is the common name for the "Society of Friends" founded by George Fox (1624-1681) in England. Their service is a silent gathering of Friends, meditating and waiting on the call of the Spirit. Their moral standards are very strict, and most are "absolute pacifists": that is, they do not recognize warfare or hostility as a means of settling human affairs, and they actively campaign against it. They are noted for their charitable work, especially for their Relief Societies which channel charity to victims of war. The term *Quaker* comes from a reply made by George Fox to an English judge in which he told him to "quake [that is, tremble] at the word of God." Once used in derision for the Society of Friends, it was adopted by them as a term of honor. Quakers do not generally consider themselves as Protestants, but as a "third way": that is, they differ from Roman Catholics on Church authority, and from Protestants in reliance on the Bible. They rely on "fellowship in the Spirit."

The Salvation Army. Best known by "its Christmas bell ringers," the Salvation Army consists of a group of Christians committed to positive Christian action through specific works of charity directed at the very poor, the downtrodden, derelicts, and the forgotten, through working in the areas in which these people are found. It was organized on a military basis (hence, Army) by William Booth, a Methodist minister, in England in 1865. It has no dogmas, no rituals, and no set form of worship. Its reason for existence is to serve the poor. It operates in ninety-one countries in hospitals, welfare missions, half-way houses, homes for unwed pregnant girls, employment agencies, counselling centers, mobile kitchens, and a host of centers set up to meet the needs of the poor, whatever they may be.

There are other small religious groups that exert some influence on

North American society, but the influence is marginal and mostly local. Such groups range from the esoteric Baha'ism, whose founder, Baha'ullah, syncretized elements of Islam with other religions to emphasize humanity's spiritual unity, and Rosicrucianism (the Ancient and Mystical Order Rosae Crucis), a mystical religion which promises to open up the secrets of the ages to its devotees, to the Nation of Islam (Black Muslims), an Islam-derived religion for American Blacks, the various **Zen**-Buddhist groups offering peace and mental security to their practitioners, and the Amish, a strict

Mennonite group adhering to seventeenth century customs and religious practices in Pennsylvania, Ohio, Indiana, Iowa, and some parts of Canada.

Finally, the religious scene in North America is filled with religious and pseudo-religious cults of every description founded by charismatic leaders who promise salvation, peace, unity, fellowship, self-fulfillment, and spiritual rejuvenation. Most have a basis in Oriental mystical experiences and bring together elements of many different beliefs, religious practices, worship forms, and life-styles. There are about 4.5 million cult members in North America spread among four hundred different groups in Mexico, the United States, and Canada. Most cults last only during the lifetime of their founders.

The most widely known groups outside of the primitive religions, and some European off-shoots of established religions, are the Unification Church of Sun Myung Moon, with about 30,000 members (called "Moonies"); Transcendental Meditation adherents, who combine practices of Hinduism with **Tantra Yoga** in an essentially non-denominational system, and have their own **"mantra,"** or secret sound, with about 360,000 practitioners most of whom have not changed their religious affiliations or beliefs; the Children of God (nicknamed "Jesus Freaks"), who believe in an immanent world war, followed by a return of Jesus who will show people how to love, with perhaps 8000 members in the United States and Canada; the Church of Scientology, founded in 1950 by Lafayette Ronald Hubbard, a science fiction writer, whose nearly two million members believe that humans are descended from ancient gods, called "Thetans," and that they can shed the accumulation of mental block they inherit by secret words and practices; and the International Society of Krishna Consciousness, or Hari Krishna, a religion derived from Hinduism, whose members preach their love-religion on street corners, in airports, train and bus stations, with about 15,000 members in the United States and Canada.

Although all of the groups mentioned in this chapter are not so large or so influential in North American life as the more prominent groups mentioned earlier, all of them represent for their members an important and personal relationship with God. Like the people in the larger religious groups, they, too, are responding to the Mystery of life in a way that makes sense to them.

A Final Word

In any discussion about religion, the question of atheism arises. An atheist is a person who does not believe in a God because he says it cannot be proved that there is a God.

A person might wonder why, in a book discussing religion, the question of atheism is raised. It is raised for three reasons. First, atheists take a position relative to religion and its practices; therefore, a discussion of atheism is relevant. Second, most religious people ask themselves from time to time whether or not the contention of atheists that there is no God is true; therefore, the question of atheism is relevant to them. Third, if the definition used in this book to describe what religion is is correct, then atheism is religion. In North America, there are about two million atheists.

Atheism may be regarded as a religion because it is a response to the mystery of life and because, like God-oriented responses, it is a belief. Its belief is that there is no God; its response is that of life practices based on that belief.

The purpose of this book has been not to prove or disprove the existence of God, to judge the validity of people's response to whatever God is for them, or to approve or disapprove the religious practices of people who respond in their own way to whatever God is for them. Its purpose has been to present a panoramic view of the beliefs and religious practices of the people of North America and to help its readers understand the beliefs and religious practices of those among whom they live. We hope these purposes have been accomplished in *Religion in North America*.

For Review and Discussion

1. What is the origin of the word *Jew*? Of *Judaism*? Of *Israel*? Who are the Israelis?
2. What is a *Jew*? Make a distinction among the three expressions of Judaism.
3. What is the Bible for Jews? How does it differ from the Christian Bible? What is the Torah?
4. What is an Eastern Orthodox Christian? What was the real cause for the separation of the Christian Church into Eastern and Western segments?
5. What is the proper name for the religion commonly called "Mormonism"? Why is it so called? Why do outsiders call it "Mormonism"?
6. With what particular practice is each of the following religions identified: Christian Science, Jehovah's Witnesses, Seventh-Day Adventism, the Society of Friends (Quakers), the Salvation Army, the Nation of Islam?
7. Discuss whether or not atheism is a religion.
8. Be sure you can define the following:

agnostic	Mormon
Amish	Orthodox
atheist	Patriarchate
baptism for the dead	Quaker
Bar Mitzvah	rabbi
celestial marriage	Sabbath
Christian Scientist	sacrament
cult	synagogue
Eastern Orthodox	tithe
iconostas	Torah
Jehovah's Witnesses	Yahweh

For Research

1. Find out the origin of the name *Palestine* and of the designations BCE and CE in the Jewish calendar.
2. Research the history of the origin and content of the Jewish Bible.
3. Find out about, and report on, what "smaller" Church groups may exist in your area.
4. Prepare a report on some modern religious cult you may have heard about recently.
5. If you can, attend a religious service of one of the groups mentioned in this chapter other than your own, if any. Be prepared to report your observations to the class.
6. Research Mother Ann Lee and the Shakers, Oneida, Brook Farm, Amana, New Harmony, or one of the other "ideal communities" founded in the nineteenth century in North America.

Bibliography

Chapter One: The Present State of Religion in North America

1. *Religion in America.* The Gallup Opinion Index 1978. Princeton, New Jersey: The American Institute of Public Opinion, 1978.
2. *Readers' Digest Almanac and Yearbook 1978.* Pleasantville, New York: The Readers' Digest Association, 1978.
3. *World Almanac and Book of Facts, 1978.* New York: Newspaper Enterprise Association, 1978.
4. *The Denominational Society.* Andrew Greeley. Glenview, Illinois: Scott, Foresman and Company, 1973.
5. *Protestant, Catholic, Jew.* Will Herberg. Garden City, New York: Doubleday & Company, 1955.
6. *Religions of America.* Leo Rosten, ed. New York: Simon & Schuster, 1975.
7. *Protestantism.* Martin E. Marty. New York: Holt, Rinehart, Winston, 1972.
8. *Religion in Canada.* William Kilbourn, ed. Toronto: McClelland & Stewart, 1968.
9. *The Modern Schism.* Martin E. Marty. Evanston, Illinois: Harper & Row, 1967.
10. *Life After Life.* Raymond E. Moody, Jr., MD. New York: Bantam Books, 1976.
11. *Our Brothers in Christ.* Henri Daniel-Rops. New York: E. P. Dutton & Company, 1967.
12. *Encyclopedia of American Religions.* J. Gordon Melton. Wilmington, North Carolina: Consortium Books, 1979.

Chapter Two: The Religion of the Earliest Americans

1. *The American Heritage Book of Indians.* William Brandon. New York: The American Heritage Publishing Company, 1961.
2. *The First Americans.* [The Emergence of Man Series.] Robert Claiborne. New York: Time-Life Publications, 1973.
3. *The Hawaiians.* Norfork Island, Australia: Island Heritage Ltd. 1970.
4. *American Indian Mythology.* Alice Marriott and Carol K. Rachlin. New York: Thomas Y. Crowell, 1968.
5. *America's First Civilization.* Michael D. Coe. New York: The American Heritage Publishing Company, 1968.
6. *Clues to America's Past.* Washington, DC: The National Geographic Society, 1976.
7. *The People's Almanac.* David Wallechinsky and Irving Wallace. Garden City, New York: Doubleday & Company, 1975.
8. *Non-Christian Religions A to Z.* Horace L. Friess, ed. New York: Grosset & Dunlop, 1963.

Chapter Three: Roman Catholicism in North America

1. *America's Beginnings.* Tee Loftin Snell. Washington, DC: The National Geographic Society, 1974.
2. *Religions of America.* Leo Rosten, ed. New York: Simon & Schuster, 1975.
3. *American Catholicism.* John Tracy Ellis. Chicago: University of Chicago Press, 1963.
4. *The Church of Apostles and Martyrs.* Henri Daniel-Rops. Garden City, New York: Doubleday & Company, 1962.
5. *Yearbook of American and Canadian Churches 1977.* Constant H. Jacquet. Nashville, Tennessee: Abingdon Press, 1977.
6. *The Christian Church in Canada.* H. H. Walsh. Toronto: Ryerson Press, 1956.
7. *Religion in Canada.* William Kilbourn, ed. Toronto: McClelland & Stewart, 1968.
8. *What Americans Believe and How They Worship.* J. Paul Williams. Evanston, Illinois: Harper & Row, 1962.
9. *The Age of Faith.* Anne Fremantle. New York: Time, Inc., 1965.
10. *The Reformation.* Edith Simon. New York: Time, Inc., 1966.
11. *The Emerging Church.* Ronald J. Wilkins. Dubuque, Iowa: Wm. C. Brown Company Publishers, 1975.
12. *The Counter Reformation.* Arthur G. Dickins. New York: Harcourt Brace Jovanovich, 1969.

Chapter Four: Protestantism in North America

1. *The Protestant Reformation.* Henri Daniel-Rops. Garden City, New York: Doubleday & Company, 1961.
2. *The Reformation.* Edith Simon. New York: Time, Inc. 1966.
3. *A Handbook of Christian Theology.* Marvin Halberson and Arthur Cohen, eds. Cleveland: World Publishing Company, 1967.
4. *Religions of America.* Leo Rosten, ed. New York: Simon & Schuster, 1975.
5. *Great Religions of the World.* Washington, DC: The National Geographic Society, 1971.
6. *The Religions of Man.* Huston Smith. New York: Harper & Row, 1965.
7. *The Modern Reader's Guide to Religions.* Harold H. Watts. New York: Barnes & Noble, 1965.
8. *Our Brothers in Christ.* Henri Daniel-Rops. New York: E. P. Dutton & Company, 1967.
9. *Understanding Protestantism.* Georges Tavard. Glen Rock, New Jersey: Paulist Press, 1964.
10. *The Religions of the World.* William J. Whalen. Chicago: Claretian Publications, 1977.
11. *Protestantism.* J. Leslie Dunston. New York: George Braziller, 1962.
12. *Protest Dictionary: Containing Articles on the History, Doctrines & Practices of the Christian Church.* Charles Wright and Charles Neill, eds. Detroit, Michigan: Gale Research, Inc., 1971.
13. *Protestant Faith.* George W. Forell. Philadelphia: Fortress Press, 1971.
14. *Protestantism in America: a Narrative History.* Jerold C. Brauer. Philadelphia: Westminster Press, 1972.

15. *Righteous Empire: the Protestant Experience in America.* Martin E. Marty. New York: Dial Press, 1970.
16. *The Spirit of Protestantism.* Robert McAfee Brown. New York: Oxford University Press, 1965.
17. *Protestantism.* Martin E. Marty. New York: Holt, Rinehart, Winston, 1972.
18. *The Christian Church in Canada.* H. H. Walsh. Toronto: Ryerson Press, 1956.
19. *Religion in Canada.* William Kilbourn, ed. Toronto: McClelland & Stewart, 1968.

Chapter Five: The Principal Protestant Denominations in North America

1. *Religions of America.* Leo Rosten, ed. New York: Simon & Schuster, 1975.
2. *The Reformation.* Edith Simon. New York: Time, Inc., 1966.
3. *A Handbook of Christian Theology.* Marvin Halberson and Arthur Cohen, eds. Cleveland: World Publishing Company, 1967.
4. *The Church in the Eighteenth Century.* Henri Daniel-Rops. Garden City, New York: Doubleday & Company, 1966.
5. *Our Brothers in Christ.* Henri Daniel-Rops. New York: E. P. Dutton & Company, 1967.
6. *Great Religions of the World.* Washington, DC: The National Geographic Society, 1971.
7. *Yearbook of American and Canadian Churches* 1977. Constant A. Jacquet. Nashville, Tennessee: Abingdon Press, 1977.
8. *Protestant Churches of America.* John A. Hardin. Garden City, New York: Doubleday & Company, 1969.
9. *Protestant Christianity Interpreted through Its Development.* John Dillenger and Claude Welch. New York: Charles Scribner's Sons, 1954.
10. *The Protestant Crusade: 1800–1860.* Ray A. Billington. New York: Quadrangle Press, 1964.
11. *Protestantism.* Martin E. Marty. New York: Holt, Rinehart, Winston, 1972.
12. *What Americans Believe and How They Worship.* J. Paul Williams. New York: Harper & Row, 1962.
13. *The Christian Church in Canada.* H. H. Walsh. Toronto: Ryerson Press, 1956.
14. *Religion in Canada.* William Kilbourn, ed. Toronto: McClelland & Stewart, 1968.

Baptist:

15. *Short History of the Baptists.* H. C. Vedder. Valley Forge, Pennsylvania: Judson Press, 1949.
16. *A Way Home: the Baptists Tell Their Story.* James S. Childers, ed. New York: Holt, Rinehart, Winston, 1964.
17. *My Church.* J. B. Moody. Greenwood, North Carolina: Attic Press, 1974.

Presbyterian:

18. *Our Presbyterian Heritage.* Paul Carlson. Elgin, Illinois: David C. Cook, 1973.
19. *A Brief History of the Presbyterians.* Lefferts Loetscher. Philadelphia: Westminster Press, 1958.

Methodist:

20. *A New Adventure in the Meaning of United Methodist Membership.* Ron Kerr. Nashville, Tennessee: Tydings, 1969.

21. *Membership Means Discipleship*. Wayne Clymer. Nashville, Tennessee: Tydings, 1976.
22. *Essential United Methodist Beliefs*. James Hares. Nashville, Tennessee: Tydings, *n.d.*
23. *Beliefs of a United Methodist Christian*. Emerson Colaw. Nashville, Tennessee: Tydings, *n.d.*

Episcopalian:
24. *The Church of England and the American Episcopal Church*. H. G. G. Herklots. London: A. R. Mowbray & Company, Ltd., 1966.
25. *An Approach to the Episcopal Church*. Carroll E. Simcox. New York: Morehouse-Barlow Company, 1963.
26. *The Episcopalian's Dictionary*. Howard Harper. New York: The Seabury Press, 1974.

Lutheran:
27. *The Lutheran Church in North America*. E. Clifford Nelson. Philadelphia: Fortress Press, 1975.
28. *The Lutheran Church Past and Present*. Vilmos Vajta. Minneapolis: Augsburg Publishing House, 1977.
29. *The Church of the Lutheran Reformation*. Conrad Bergendorff. St. Louis, Missouri: Concordia Press, 1967.
30. *The Legacy of Luther*. Ernest Walter Zeeden. Westminster, Maryland: Newman Press, 1954.

Chapter Six: Other Influential Religious Groups in North America
1. *Jews, God and History*. Max I. Dimont. New York: New American Library, 1964.
2. *The Israelites*. New York: Time-Life Books, 1975.
3. *Introduction to Judaism*. Lee A. Belford. New York: Association Press/Scott, Foresman and Company, 1961.
4. *Jerusalem*. Jerusalem, Israel: Keter Publishing House, 1973.
5. *Judaism, Profile of a Faith*. Ben Zion Bokser. New York: Alfred A. Knopf 1963.
6. *Jewish Heritage Reader*. Lily Edelman, ed. New York: Toplinger Publishing Company, 1965.
7. *The Mormons*. Thomas F. O'Dea. Chicago: University of Chicago Press, 1965.
8. *Religions of America*. Leo Rosten, ed. New York: Simon & Schuster, 1975.
9. *Faiths for the Few*. William J. Whalen. Milwaukee, Wisconsin: Bruce Publishing Company, 1963.
10. *Our Brothers in Christ*. Henri Daniel-Rops. New York: E. P. Dutton & Company, 1967.
11. *Churches in North America*. Gustave Weigel, S.J. Baltimore: Helicon Press, 1961.
12. *What Americans Believe and How They Worship*. J. Paul Williams. Evanston, Illinois: Harper & Row, 1962.
13. *Religion in Canada*. William Kilbourn, ed. Toronto: McClelland & Stewart, 1968.

Glossary

Acts of the Apostles—the New Testament book attributed to Luke, which describes the origin and development of the early Christian church.

Agnostic—one who is uncertain of God's existence, or holds God unknowable.

Amerind—anthropological designation for a native American.

Amish—followers of Jacob Amman, seventeenth century Swiss Mennonite bishop, who hold to absolute separation of church and state, non-violence, and utilitarian living.

Amulet—ornament imbued with magic to aid wearer.

Anabaptist—Protestant who believes in adult baptism by immersion, a concept popular since the sixteenth century.

Anglican—one who is in communion with the Church of England. "Anglican" came from the Latin word *angli*, used to designate the people of England.

Anglo-Catholic—name given to that section of the Anglican communion which claims complete continuity from the pre-Reformation Catholic church in England.

Animism—belief that a soul inhabits *every* living being.

Apostle—from the Greek word *apostolos*, meaning "one who is sent." One of the twelve men selected by Jesus to be his principal emissaries in preaching Christianity. They were Peter, John, Andrew, James the Greater, James the Less, Jude, Simon, Matthew, Nathaniel Bartholomew, Simon, Thomas, and Matthias, who replaced Judas. Paul was later called an apostle because of his work throughout the Mediterranean area.

Apostle's Creed—a summary of Christian belief dating back to the sixth century; it is traditionally ascribed to Christ's apostles.

Astrology—the divination of the supposed influences of the stars and planets on human affairs by their positions and aspects.

Athanasian Creed—a statement of faith attributed to Athanasius, bishop of Alexandria in Egypt; it dates from around 400 AD.

Atheist—one who denies the existence of God.

Augsburg Confession—a statement of belief and doctrine as formulated by Philip Melancthon (1497–1560), a theologian and associate of Martin Luther. It was presented at the Diet of Augsburg, Germany, in 1530, and became the principal statement of belief, or creed, of all Lutheran churches. Melancthon hoped to reconcile Protestantism with Catholicism, and thus to restore Christian unity.

Autonomous—self-governing.

Avatar—visible manifestation.

Aztecs—an Amerindian tribe of central Mexico, who founded an empire conquered by Cortez in 1519.

Baptism—a Christian sacrament by which a person is initiated into the mystery of the Christian community, via a ceremony involving immersion in, or pouring on of, water.

Baptism for the Dead—Mormon practice of receiving baptism in the name of someone dead, to insure the deceased's redemption.

Bar Mitzvah— "Son of the Law," the ceremony in which Jewish boys assume adult responsibility in the sight of the community. An equivalent ceremony for girls is the *bas mitzvah*.

"Before Christ"—a system of dating history based on the birth of Christ, developed by Dionysius Exiquus, a sixth century monk. Dates were designated BC or AD [*anno domini*, "in the year of Our Lord"]. Before that, dates were determined by the beginning of the reign of the current Roman Emperor, or from the founding of Rome in 753 BC, and were expressed AUB [*ab urbe condita*, "from the founding of the city"].

Beringia Bridge—prehistoric land mass linking Alaska with Siberia.

Bible—the collection of sacred writings of Judaism and Christianity; the partial record of a religious interpretation of real history.

Bishop—one who has authority over other clergy.

Book of Common Prayer—official Anglican prayer book.

Cahokia—a large, well-developed Amerindian Mound Builder city, which flourished in southern Illinois about 1100 AD. It dominated an area approximately the size of New York state.

Calvinist—follower of John Calvin (1509–64); one who believes God predestines some to damnation before any consideration of their sins.

Canonize—in the Roman Catholic Church, to formally declare the person in question a saint.

Cardinal—a high ecclesiastical official, usually a bishop, appointed to the Roman Catholic college of cardinals by the Pope.

Catholic—from the Greek word *katholikos*, meaning "universal"; now applied mainly to a member of the Roman Catholic Church.

Celestial Marriage—in Mormon belief, a marriage which continues in heaven as well as on earth.

Charism—according to Christian belief, a divinely conferred gift given to an individual for the good of the community or the spread of the Christian message.

Charismatic—one who possesses a charism, such as prophecy, faith, speaking in tongues, wisdom, healing, and the like.

Christian Science—religion founded by Mary Baker Eddy (1821–1910), which rejects medicine, holding that all illness can be healed by belief and prayer.

Circuit Rider—a clergyman assigned to a regular tour around a designated territory for the purpose of holding religious services at churches therein.

Clerical—pertaining to someone who has been designated a member of the clergy.

Communion—union of all Christians with Christ;

also, in some churches, the sacrament by which believers receive spiritual nourishment.

Congregationalism—form of organization adopted by certain Protestants in England under Elizabeth I: each body of worshippers is independent of all others.

Conquistador—a leader in the Spanish conquest of the Americas in the sixteenth century.

Conservative Jew—one who adheres for the most part to the orthodox principles and practices of Judaism, but who modifies them according to circumstances.

Contemplation—private spiritual or mystical thought.

Covenant—an agreement or testament between two parties.

Convention—a group of Baptist churches belonging to an association with common aims, purposes, goals, and general theology.

Creed—an official formula of religious belief.

Cult—a small religious group outside of the established church group, or regarded as unorthodox within it.

Deacon—subordinate officer in a Christian church.

Deist—one who holds to a religion based on human reason, not divine revelation.

Denomination—a religious organization comprised of a number of local congregations.

Diet—a formal deliberative assembly of European princes

Divination—the practice of attempting to tell the future or to discover hidden knowledge by magical means.

Doctrine—a principle in a system of belief.

Dogmas—church doctrines, formally stated and authoritatively proclaimed.

Eastern Orthodox—see Orthodox Christian.

Ecstacy—condition, resulting from high state of prayer, in which reason and self-control are suspended.

Ecumenism—movement toward Christian unity.

Episcopal—pertaining to a bishop.

Epistles—New Testament letters written to the early Christian communities.

Esoteric—not simple, not for the unlettered.

Eucharist—from the Greek for "thanksgiving," another name for the Roman Catholic and/or Anglican sacrament of Communion; among Christian Scientists, spiritual communion with God.

Evangelical—the name given to those who hold that the Bible alone contains the rule of faith, to be interpreted privately.

Excommunication—the declaration by church authority that a person no longer belongs to the community or shares in its spiritual blessings.

Exodus—Old Testament book detailing the departure of the Israelites from Egypt to the Promised Land.

Faith—belief, trust, and loyalty to a god and/or religion; also, acceptance based on the testimony of reliable witnesses.

Fetishism—belief in the power of magical charms or superstitious objects.

Freethinker—one who doubts religious teaching or authority.

Fundamentalism—a movement or attitude stressing a strict or literal interpretation of the Bible.

Genesis—the first book of the Old Testament, containing accounts of creation and the origin of the Jewish people.

Glossolaliacal—characterized by speaking in incomprehensible sounds.

Gospels—from the Old English word *Godspell,* meaning "good news"—the accounts of Christ's life and teachings attributed to the four evangelists: Matthew, Mark, Luke, and John.

Hierarchy—a ruling body organized in levels of rank, with each level subordinate to the level above it.

Holy Roman Empire—an empire made up of the territory of the western part of the original Roman Empire. It was the territory ruled first by Charlemagne, King of France, who was crowned emperor by Pope Leo III in 800 AD. It was called "holy" to signify that it was Christian. The title later went to individual nobles who were crowned emperor by the reigning Pope. The title was conferred upon various European royalty until the Holy Roman Empire came to an end in 1806, but by that time it was largely symbolic. It was abandoned by Francis I, Emperor of Austria, to prevent the conqueroring Napoleon Bonaparte from assuming its crown.

Humanist—one who focuses thought and culture on the natural perfectability of humankind, often rejecting supernaturalism.

Ice Age—the Pleistocene glacial epoch.

Iconography—pictorial material, including traditional symbols or images, relating to a particular subject.

Iconostasis—a screen, adorned with icons (religious images), separating the sanctuary from the nave in Byzantine rite churches.

Immanent—in Judeo-Christian belief, a term used to describe a God who is in touch with people to whom he reveals himself and whom he is saving in their lives as they live them.

Indulgence—according to Roman Catholic belief, a partial or complete remission of the temporal punishment due to sin.

Jehovah's Witnesses—a group that witnesses by personal evangelism to the rule of God, the sinfulness of the world, and the Second Coming.

Judaism—the religion of the Jewish people, characterized by belief in one God and the living out of his law as expressed in their scripture.

Justification by faith—a principal doctrine of Lutheranism: people are saved not through their own actions but solely through the goodness of God.

Literal Interpretation—in some Protestant churches, the acceptance of every word of the Bible as fact.

Liturgy—official, public ceremonies of worship; [when capitalized] often used to refer to a eucharistic rite, that is, a celebration of the Lord's Supper—the celebration of the last Passover meal by Jesus with his disciples before he was crucified.

Lord's Supper—Communion; the Eucharist.

Lutheran—follower of Martin Luther (1483-1546), holding to the doctrines Luther developed, such as justification by faith, vernacular liturgy, priority of conscience and scripture, priesthood of the laity, and so on.

Magic—supposed supernatural influence over natural objects.

Mana—Polynesian concept of a "power."

Mantra—in Hinduism, a prayer, invocation, or incantation associated with meditation.

Mass—principal act of Catholic worship, centered around the celebration of the Eucharist.

Materialist—one who believes that nothing spiritual exists.

Maya—a large tribe of Amerinds living in southern Mexico and north central America, who flourished from about 60 AD to 800 AD.

Mennonite—follower of Menno Simons (1492-1559). Each Mennonite congregation is autonomous; they all reject military service, holding to separation of church and state, and are best-known for their simple life-style.

Mesoamerica—central America from the middle of Mexico to central Honduras.

Messiah—Hebrew form of the Greek name *Christ,* meaning "one who is anointed"; the prophesied king of Israel, long-awaited by the Jews.

Methodist—follower of John Wesley (1703-91), who stresses personal and social morality.

Millenium—reign of Christ on earth, the "Second Coming," which according to the Book of Revelation will last 1000 years.

Minister—one who administers a sacrament, usually a clergyman; also, a clergyman, especially of a Protestant communion.

Miracle—an extraordinary action by which God enables his saving powers to be recognized.

Monk—member of religious order devoted to the contemplative life, bound by vows.

Moral—conforming to a right standard of behavior.

Mormon—member of the Church of Jesus Christ of the Latter-day Saints.

Mystery—in Eastern Orthodoxy, an action of God in his church designed to bring about holiness among his people. Eastern Orthodox sacraments differ from other mysteries—or holy actions, in their history, nature, purpose, and intent.

Mystical—having a spiritual meaning or reality apparent to neither reason or the senses.

Myth—story or tradition, often with some historical basis, which demonstrates the worldview of a particular people.

Nicene Creed—formal statement of Christian belief adopted at the First Council of Nicea in 325 A.D.

Many Protestant denominations, as well as Roman Catholic and Eastern Orthodox churches, use this creed for the expression of what they believe. They may differ, however, in understanding what some of the expressions in this creed mean.

Nun—woman belonging to a religious order, usually in a cloister.

Olmec—Ameindian tribe living in Mexico from around 100 B.C. to 300 A.D.

Orthodox—from the Greek word *ortho,* meaning "correct," and *doxa,* meaning "opinion" or "view"; conforming to established doctrine.

Orthodox Christian—member of an Eastern Christian church, separated from Rome. These churches include, generally, all those allied with the Patriarch of Constantinople.

Orthodox Jew—one who adheres faithfully to the traditional principles and practices of Judaism.

Pantheism—the belief that all the universe is God.

Papist—one who supports the Pope; spec., a Roman Catholic.

Passover—the Jewish feast commemorating Hebrew liberation from slavery in Egypt.

Patriarch—head of a rite within the Christian church, usually in Roman Catholicism or Eastern Orthodoxy. The Pope is the Patriarch of the West. Also, the head of an Eastern Orthodox church.

Pentateuch—the first five books of the Bible [*see also* Torah].

Pentecost—the Christian feast which celebrates the descent of the Holy Spirit upon the apostles.

Pentecostal—believing in direct inspiration by the Holy Spirit.

Polynesian—a member of the native peoples of Polynesia, the islands of the central Pacific.

Polytheism—belief in many gods.

Pope—Catholic bishop of Rome, head of the Roman Catholic Church, considered by his followers the successor to St. Peter, leader of Christ's apostles—from the Greek word, *pappas,* meaning "father."

Pragmatic—practical; disposed to action as opposed to speculation.

Predestination—Calvinist teaching that God wills the damnation of some souls, the salvation of others.

Presbyterial—from the Greek word *presbyteros,* meaning "elder"; placing authority in the hands of a presbytery composed of a minister together with lay elders.

Presbytery—in Presbyterian churches, a ruling body consisting of the ministers and representative elders within a district.

Primacy of jurisdiction—the principle that the pope ranks first in the order of rank and power in the governing aspect of the Roman Catholic church.

Primacy of the Bible—the principle that the New Testament is to be treated as the standard, or norm, of Christian faith.

Prophet—one through whom God reveals himself.

Protestant—from the Latin word *protestari,*

meaning "to declare publicly"—a member of one of the Christian churches that separated from Rome at the time of the Reformation.

Puberty rites—ceremonies marking the coming of age of children.

Puritan—one who held scripture to be the sole authority for faith, and who rejected all externals in worship; an offshoot of Anglicanism which developed in Reformation England.

Quaker—a member of the Society of Friends, founded by George Fox in 1668; their most famous attribute is absolute opposition to all forms of violence and injustice.

Quasi-religious—resembling religion.

Rabbi—a Jew qualified to expound upon and interpret the Torah.

Rationalist—one who relies on reason as the basis for determining religious truths.

Reform Jew—a Jew who practices a system of ethics and religious rituals which are meaningful in light of contemporary conditions.

Reincarnation—rebirth in new forms of earthly life

Religion—the human response to whatever the answer to the mystery of life is for a person.

Religious—a man or woman bound by vows and devoted to a life of piety.

Religious pluralism—a society in which diverse religious groups participate autonomously.

Revelation—knowledge given by God concerning himself.

Rite—prescribed actions and words of worship; also, in Roman Catholicism a system of liturgical worship approved by the church, for example, the Latin rite, Byzantine rite, and so on.

Ritual—practices or traditions relating to religion and worship.

Sabbath—a day set aside for religious worship; specifically, from Friday evening to Saturday evening for Jews, and Sunday for most Christians.

Sacrament—a formal religious act, sacred as a sign of spiritual reality.

Saints—meaning "holy ones," is a word that many New Testament writers used to signify the members of the church of Jesus. It is so used by the Mormons. Saints in the Roman Catholic Church are any whose holiness of life and contribution to the church has been deemed extraordinary and so declared by the official church.

Salvation—in Christian belief, the act of being saved from sin by Jesus Christ.

Scripture—the sacred writings of a religion.

Second Coming—anticipated return to earth by Jesus Christ.

Secular—worldly, or without regard to religious elements.

Seder—Passover dinner; *seder* means "order."

Shaman—one who acts as both priest and doctor, working with the supernatural.

Sin—according to Christian belief, any thought, word, act, or failure to act which alienates a person from

God. "To save from sin" means to deliver from the power and consequences of sin. Christians believe that Jesus came not only to deliver individuals from the power and consequences of moral evil, but also to free the world from the power and consequences of moral evil. They believe he did this by his presence and by his teaching, which enabled people to free themselves from the power and consequences of moral evil with God's help.

Sister—member of a religious community of women.

Swami—Hindu religious teacher.

Synagogue—Jewish building for religious services, from the Greek word for the "gathering of people."

Synod—an ecclesiastical governing or advisory council.

Taboo—forbidden; from the Polynesian word for "negative force."

Talmud—authoritative collection of Jewish tradition.

Tantric—branch of Buddhism which incorporates magic rituals and polytheism.

Theocracy—government by avowed representatives of God.

Thesis—a statement, or proposition, put forward for discussion or debate. Posting notices on church doors, as in the case of Luther's ninety-five theses, was a common practice in medieval Europe. The church door was a kind of community bulletin board.

Tithe—giving, yearly, one-tenth of one's income to a church.

Torah—the collection of law in Jewish Scripture, including the Pentateuch: Genesis, Exodus, Leviticus, Numbers and Deuteronomy.

Totemism—belief in kinship and/or patronage of a revered symbol.

Transcend—as a noun, that attribute of the Judeo-Christian God which means beyond, above, and outside of the world of people, and not controlled by them, as the gods of other peoples could supposedly be by magic.

Transmigration—the movement of the soul at death from one being or body to another.

Tribe—a social group comprising numerous related clans together with dependents.

Trinity—Three Persons in One God: Father, Son and Holy Spirit. A belief held by most Christians.

Unitarian—a rationalist who believes in the unity of all things.

United Church of Canada—a union of the majority of the Methodist, Presbyterian, and Congregational churches into the largest Protestant denomination in Canada, formed in 1925.

Vow—a promise freely made to God.

Yahweh—the God of the Hebrews; the name given by him to the Israelites, according to the Book of Exodus.

Yoga—a system of physical discipline designed to achieve a spiritual purpose.

Zen—major division of Buddhism in which, under the direction of a master teacher, one attempts to arrive at Satori—the moment of truth.

Index